DRIVING
FORWARD
IN REVERSE

50 Car Metaphors for Counselors, Teachers, and Life Coaches to Help Others Navigate Life

JOHN MCCARTHY, PH.D.
ALONG WITH MELISSA LAKE, M.A.

ISBN 978-1-939237-84-2

Published by Suncoast Digital Press, Inc.
Sarasota, Florida, U.S.A.

Contents

Preface

It was my second week in my first post-doctoral position in 1995. I was an assistant professor in Counseling at St. Bonaventure University. My office phone rang. "Hi, this is Barbara Carr," the person on the other end said. "We have a mutual friend, and I wanted to welcome you to St. Bonaventure. When can we have lunch?" Her voice was somehow uplifting, filled with joy, energy, and fervor. She and I planned to meet the following week, and my experience of her rang consistent with my first impression.

Barbara was one of the development officers at the University, and, as I learned through time, she was well respected by all. She embodied optimism, joy, dedication, and a strong sense of spirituality. Easy to be with along with a good sense of humor and wonderment about life, Barbara had a *way* of being with people. It was difficult not to like Barbara. She greeted people with a smile, exuberance, and respect.

Barbara and I became good friends over time. About 15 months into our friendship, she called me to tell me that she had been diagnosed with breast cancer. Consistent with her nature, she discussed it an upbeat tone that personified hope.

A Saturday morning talk over coffee with Barbara produced the title of this book. In our bantering, we talked about a road where, if a car were put into neutral, it seems to magically go uphill. Somehow out of this came the phrase "going forward in reverse." I recall saying, "Yes! *Going forward in reverse.* That would make an excellent title for a book." And so it is, in large part due to Barbara.

Tragically, Barbara's cancer ended her life in 2003. She lived with a profound passion, and it is in her memory that I entitle this book.

Introduction

I once attended a wonderful workshop given by Bill O'Hanlon, author of many books on various aspects of counseling and therapy. The seminar was about solution-focused therapy, and he told his story of how he learned and developed his skills. The critical word in that last sentence is "story." He discussed his work in Milwaukee and how the community counseling center had decided to contact counselors' former clients to determine what they had obtained from their experience at the center. When it came to O'Hanlon's former clients, they indicated that they remembered his stories. Yes, the stories that he told in counseling for various goals: to make a point; to confront the person, or perhaps to empower the client. "And," he added, "that's what you'll probably take from this workshop today: the stories that I tell." In my case, he was right. His stories made the day.

Metaphors, to me, are similar to stories. They put something in pictures, and for those who think in images, this seemingly small intervention can be quite profound. Metaphors are brief, yet can be memorable guides to driving your life. They are also something which can be acted out—even role played—in a counseling session. Metaphors represent something that can be *taken* from a session and "lived" outside of the counseling office. Finally, they can also be used for the basis of a homework assignment.

So why cars? In 2000, I wrote an article in *Counseling Today*, the monthly publication for members of the American Counseling Association, entitled "Drivers' education = Counseling techniques?" (McCarthy, 2000). The article discussed the similarity between learning how to drive a car and various counseling processes and interventions. That was an impetus for this book, as it dawned on me that many more illustrations could be made and expanded into a book about driving and counseling.

Face it, we are all taking a journey in life, and you're driving in life—and you have inevitably hit some speed bumps along the way. Cars represent life's journey in a multitude of ways. Consider the following from the U.S. Department of Transportation (2018):

1. The US had more than 269 million registered vehicles.

2. Those cars drive over three trillion miles a year.

3. They drive on 48,000 miles of interstate highways and, as of 2017, over 615,000 bridges throughout the country. (The states with the most bridges? Texas and Ohio.)

4. On average, drivers added a bit over 10,000 miles to the odometer of the car in 2017.

Like it or not, cars dominate our mode of transportation, so, people of all ages can relate to them. In the US, it is simply difficult to escape the notion of a car. I recall a young boy in my daughter's preschool classroom. Only three years old, he could name the type of car that every family drove. Three years old!

How can you use these metaphors in teaching, coaching, counseling, presenting, or growing in life? First off, remember one thing: I know next to nothing about cars, and you don't have to either in order to use this book. My knowledge is limited: Find the key to the car (sometimes a challenge for me!), insert it into the ignition, and turn. Somehow the car moves, and that's about all I know.

And yet the counseling literature is filled with references on the use of metaphors. Kopp (1995) wrote a book titled *Metaphor Therapy*, and subsequent journal articles in various sources have addressed the use of metaphors in helping clients. Tay (2012) discussed metaphor types in enhancing counseling. Genuchi, Hopper, and Morrison. (2017) addressed the use of metaphors in counseling college men. Robert and Kelly (2010) offered an extensive discussion on metaphors as instruments of change. Chesley, Gillett, and Wagner (2008) addressed the use of verbal and even nonverbal therapeutic metaphors in working with children. Finally, from the work of Storlie, Giegerich, Stoner-Harris, and Byrd (2018), it is evident that metaphors often come to counselor trainees' minds…they found over 450 metaphors from reflective journals among students in internship!

The use of metaphors abounds in counseling and can certainly relate to other professions. As an educator, an executive or life coach, a mental health professional, or a trainer, are you trying to relate a point? Add to the insight of your client/student/audience? Work in a Socratic dialogue approach in teaching a skill? Using such analogies can be highly effective.

1.   Role-play: Take one of the 50 metaphors and role-play it with the client, students, or workshop participants. Put them in the proverbial driver's seat and see how they behave when behind the wheel.

2.   Homework: You will see that the book is divided by themes that describe the essence of the metaphor. Choose a metaphor that fits for your client/student—interpersonal communication, coping skills, or self-care, for instance—and utilize it in a self-help activity in between sessions, training, or classes.

The possibilities are numerous. My hope is that you will find this book practical, adaptable, and, most of all, beneficial for students, clients, trainees, and perhaps yourself in driving your professional and personal life.

PART 1

Reflection

Identity

1. License Plate: A Name for Your Car

We may not consider them names, but license plates are identifiers for cars. Their numerals/letters appear on our registration cards and insurance cards and among the details that a police officer will record in the event of an accident. It's a way to tell specifically which of the millions of cars on the road is the one that belongs to you.

But let's go deeper. Typically, a plate is provided to a car owner with numerals/letters on it, with no say from the driver. Many states offer the option of a personalized "vanity plate" for an additional fee, a creative way to uniquely express yourself via a message to surrounding drivers. (One of my personal favorites belongs to a dear friend of mine: RAKS, for "Random Acts of Kindness.")

People often have a license plate in life. Perhaps it's a name, a unique nickname, a social media "handle," or a role-based name such as "Doc." If I were to meet you, how would you introduce yourself? Simply by your first name? Your full name? The fundamental question is, "How do you identify yourself in the world?"

Pretend for a moment that you, similar to a car, have a special plate attached to your forehead and the middle of your back. People around you can see it clearly. What is the message that you are giving to others? Open and inviting? Optimistic? Negative about the world? Bringing cheer to others? Just what is the "aura" of your "plate"?

Final Tune-up: People can have various identities; they usually change over time. The identities speak of who you are and what you represent.

Questions for Driving Your Life:

1. What is the life plate message that you show to people around you?

2. If you could change it, would you? To what?

3. How easy is it to see others' life license plates?

Fuel for Thought: We think it is easy to determine a person's emotions simply from their facial expressions, right? Perhaps not. More recent theories hold that those expressions are more of a reflection of social goals than feelings. Alan Fridlund, a researcher at the University of California at Santa Barbara, wrote, "Our faces are ways we direct the trajectory of a social interaction" (Meyers, 2018).

2. Car Models: A Self-Identifier

"Hey, I just got a new car," someone may say. Inevitably the other person would ask, "Oh, what kind?" They are not just asking about what company made the car, but more often than not, about the model. It is not enough to know whether the car is a Toyota, Honda, or Ford. Rather it's about the type of car. Was it a Camry, an Accord, or a Jeep?

Walk around a parking lot sometime and look at the names of car models. You won't find them named the "Breakdown," "Fall-apart," or "Gas-Guzzler." Who would buy a car model like that, even if the car was tested to be the most reliable vehicle on the market? "Fiesta," "Odyssey," and "Focus" sound much more appealing. It's all about perception and marketability.

What is your "name?" People have nicknames, but those are usually given by other people. This is about the model name that you would give yourself. Here is a list of possibilities:

- Go-Getter
- Dependable-Me
- CanDoIt
- FlexFast
- SteadyMate
- MovingGrooving

Remember, the name is up to you. You have a choice in how you see yourself.

Final Tune-up: Self-perception is in your control.

Questions for Driving Your Life:

1. What would be your car model name(s) *today*? Would you "buy" yourself?

2. Think about people whom you respect and admire. What car model names would you give to them?

3. Pick a car model name for yourself today that you will use tomorrow. What will it be and how will your behavior be different?

Fuel for Thought: Some cultures, such as certain Native American tribes, keep their sacred names hidden from others. If the individual encounters trauma, the secret identity is still retained and can assist in their healing (Waugaman, 2011).

3. Bumper Stickers: What Message are You Sending the World?

Whoever invented bumper stickers was truly creative. Think about their simplicity: Messages—often simple ones—sent to the world that never turn off, often stay on cars forever (whether you like it or not), and can be placed nearly anywhere on a car. Whether supporting a political candidate, a favorite sports team, or touting a life philosophy, bumper stickers can make other drivers frustrated, happy, or reflective.

If you ever bought a used—excuse me, "pre-owned"—car that had a bumper sticker that you didn't particularly like, I suspect that your first action was to remove it. Why? Who would want to drive a car that was sending a message that they didn't like? Imagine a Red Sox fan buying a car from a previous owner who proudly displayed a Yankees sticker. Or a car featuring a "Think Pink" sticker (in pink, of course) for a new owner who hated the color. Consider a person who is an atheist purchasing a car espousing a religion. Everyone realizes that a bumper sticker is a reflection of what the driver wants to publicly express.

<u>Final Tune-up</u>: Bumper stickers reflect values.

<u>Questions for Driving Your Life</u>:

1. You are in love with that used car you just bought except for the atrocious bumper sticker on it. What does it say?

2. Whew! That awful sticker has been removed and a new one has been put in its place. What does this one say?

3. What are your favorite bumper stickers? Least favorite?

<u>Fuel for Thought</u>: Researchers at Northwestern University examined the relationship between what people wore and how it affected their attitudes and behaviors, suggesting that the type of clothing we choose can make an impression upon others. In addition, it can allow us to assume characteristics of the clothes themselves, like feeling smarter or like an authority (as in a white lab coat) (Marshall, 2012).

4. Lucky Number: Do You Have One?

Many people have a special, lucky, or favorite number. Mine happens to be 41. It was the NFL Chicago Bears jersey number worn by Brian Piccolo, whose tragic story was portrayed in the movie *Brian's Song* (Kulik, 1971, 1:13). It was the first movie that I watched that truly touched me, and since watching it as a child, 41 has been one of my favorite numbers.

When it comes to cars, many numbers have special meaning and are significant to many. Think about No. 3 and the legendary race car driver Dale Earnhardt. Consider the multiple television shows or movies that had a car (or route) number in their titles. Whether the movies were real or animated, fans remember the numbers of the cars and even the kinds of the cars in various scenes. In fact, Huffman (2013) ranked the top 100 cars seen in TV shows and movies. (What is #1? Have a look at the link later in the book. If you are a car and media aficionado, you may just say, "Oh, why didn't I think of that?")

The number associated with a specific car identifies it, both quickly and easily. I admire the creative marketing involved when a car number linked to a person or idea becomes widely known.

Final Tune-up: Numbers represent a car's uniqueness. Remember that you're unique, too.

Questions for Driving Your Life:

1. What number(s) would be your car identifier? Why?

2. Envision that number on your car. Where would it be displayed? The color? Its size? How does all of this reflect or represent *you*?

3. Consider the people with whom you are closest in your life. What numbers would you give to their cars and why?

Fuel for Thought: People may not have numbers, but we do have fingerprints that serve as a unique personal identifier. As far back as 1789, scientist J.C.A. Mayers said that the same fingerprint pattern was not and could not be duplicated in any two people. For years since then, the belief has stood, but never been proven (Thompson, 2019).

5. Cruisin' on a Sunday Afternoon: And Then There are the Songs

I couldn't pass up the opportunity to mention car and driving songs here, but I'll also be discussing the car radio later. So many music artists have contributed car-themed songs to fit with American's love affair with cars and road trips. Ransom compiled his own list of the coolest car songs (Ransom, 2009), including Neil Young's "Long May You Run" and John Prine's "Automobile." And who better to write the article? Mr. Ransom was both an auto writer and a music journalist. Of course, his list included Top 40 hits such as Bruce Springsteen's "Pink Cadillac" or the Beach Boys' "Fun Fun Fun" and "Little Deuce Coupe."

And car songs aren't only for adults. The Wiggles, the amazingly popular Australian musical group that has given thousands of concerts for children, scored one of their first biggest hits with "Big Red Car." Even though my children have long outgrown their music, I can hear the song playing in the back of my mind as I write.

Final Tune-up: Songs can describe everything else in life, so why not cars, trucks, and driving?

Questions for Driving Your Life:

1. What song about cars is your favorite? How does this song reflect *you*?

2. What would be the title of the song about your car?

3. What values in you would be reflected in its lyrics?

Fuel for Thought: The first commercially available car radio was made by the Galvin brothers in 1930 and sold for $130. FM radio followed in 1952, but the first "music on demand" radio was made available when Chrysler, in 1955, offered a small turntable in its high-end models that could play 45 minutes of music on 7-inch records. This idea turned out to be a flop (Berkowitz, 2010).

Taking Stock

6. Mirrors: Need to Look Backward?

Seemingly insignificant among all the important systems in cars like transmissions and fuel, every car comes with at least three mirrors. Most drivers wouldn't give them a second thought, at least until one of them happens to get knocked off. Have you ever driven a car that was missing a side or rear-view mirror? Just how often did you look towards it, forgetting that the simple, yet critical, piece of equipment wasn't there?

These mirrors help to look backward while parking or passing another car or to find out how much space is between yours and the car behind you. While driving a car without these cues would be difficult, drivers who spend too much of their time looking at a backward-pointing mirror lose sight of where they are heading.

Here's the interesting analogy with counseling: A car's mirrors help us to see only so far back, limiting our sight to the immediate vicinity. It's certainly not as if you can see miles behind you, and the greater the distance back, the more unclear the image.

As a counselor helping a client, how important is the past and how far in the past do you want to delve? How much time do you want to spend with your client looking in those backward-pointing mirrors? Spending *too* much time looking in the rear-view mirrors of life can prove fruitless; a client dwelling on that which is in the past and thus cannot be changed can become overwhelmed with regrets and even despair. Too much focus on what they should (or shouldn't) have done in the past is, obviously, pointless.

I recall a section from a textbook on counseling specific to Reality Therapy that has resonated with me. In it, Corey (2005) wrote, "As soon as possible, therapists tell clients: Whatever has happened is over; it can't be changed. The more time we spend looking back, the more we avoid looking forward'" (p. 320). It's a wonderful line that sums up much about counseling. Also, I recall hearing a radio interview with a basketball coach who said something like, "I want to buy that used car without any mirrors because I only want to look ahead."

Final Tune-Up: Mirrors are valuable, both in driving and in life. After all, they tell us where we have been, but they are not the only useful view available

Questions for Driving Your Life:

1. How much time do you spend in life in looking in your rear-view mirrors?

2. What do you see? How far back do you look?

3. What would it be like if you didn't have those mirrors?

Fuel for Thought: Taking numerous digital pictures may decrease your ability to look back and remember events. Not only does this take you out of the present moment you seek to capture, but research has also shown that individuals may not spend much time interacting and reminiscing about the experiences viewed on their phone or camera. The brain may also be more dismissive about retaining the memory since the camera may do so instead (Henkel, 2014).

7. Mile Markers: How Close (or Far) Are You?

"Are we there yet?" All of us have heard that infamous question, often asked from a car's back seat in a slow, whining, high-pitched tone by a bored child. You may have used it yourself when you were four or five years old. (I know I did!)

When we get into the driver's seat, we most often have a destination in mind. *Where do I want to end up?* I view my destination, the end point, as a goal, and mileage signs (mile markers) are reliable in telling me how close I am to that particular goal. I don't know about you, but if I'm driving a significant distance, I think that it's fun to count down the miles as I near my destination. *An hour ago, it was 178 miles and now it's only 110 miles.* There's something gratifying in that.

Life has its share of signposts, too. In the process of earning a college degree, it's reassuring to see a cumulative GPA based on an increasing number of credits. In running my first marathon, it was comforting to see distance signs along the way (though the distance between the 25- and 26-mile marks seemed to be about 10 miles). Page numbers in a book represent a progress marker, indicating how much you've covered and how close you are to the end.

It can be refreshing to see life's mile markers and know that progress is being made and that you are closer to your goal. Sometimes people ignore the signs, only to become frustrated, and begin to think that they are simply "spinning their wheels." (See #13). Take the time to see each mileage sign and give yourself a pat on the back for getting closer to where you want to go.

Final Tune-Up: Keep an eye out for life's mile markers to reaffirm your progress toward goal completion.

Questions for Driving Your Life:

1. How many "miles" are you from your most important life goal?

2. What did you recently do to edge closer and log a few more life miles towards your desired destination?

3. At the life pace you're moving, when do you hope to reach your goal?

Fuel for Thought: The word *milestone* comes from ancient Rome, with some markers dating back to 300 B.C. Emperor Augustus placed a pillar in Rome to mark the starting point for a system of roads that all led to/from Rome. With each mile marked with a "millarium," the Latin term for "milestone," travelers would know how near or far they were from the Eternal City (Rust & Strauss, n.d.).

8. Vehicle Registration: Time for a Check-up

According to headlights.com, 14 states mandate an annual safety inspection for cars. For those living in Pennsylvania, for instance, cars must pass the inspection to get the front windshield sticker notifying approval. (I once forgot about this with my own car and am grateful to the neighbor who spotted the fact that it was past inspection!) In states with this requirement, the car goes to a garage where the tires, brakes, and who knows what else are examined for safety and wear. You breathe a sigh of relief when you hear the words, "Your car passed inspection. Everything looked okay." When it doesn't pass, however, the groans begin.

Having life "inspections" can also be beneficial. Annual physicals, for instance, can be an excellent way to detect problems, especially those that have no symptoms. Blood pressure is one such example of a condition in which a person may be unaware of potential problems. One physician told me that he learned of his dangerously high blood pressure in medical school, while he and a classmate were practicing taking each other's vital signs.

Physical exams are just one example of evaluations, though. Retreats can serve as times of mental and spiritual introspection where one can take time to consider various aspects of life. From my own experience in life, retreats can make a tremendous difference.

Final Tune-Up: Regular self-inspections or reviews can be worthwhile physically, mentally, and spiritually.

Questions for Driving Your Life:

1. When was the last time you had a physical exam?

2. What fears or anxieties hold you back from an evaluation that you are thinking about?

3. Schedule a self-inspection and take some time to think about the benefits. How might it enrich your life?

Fuel for thought: Take a quick moment to inspect your thoughts. An individual may have around 60,000 thoughts a day, many of which are the rehashing of worries and that can lead to a cluttered mind. A tip for de-cluttering the mind may be to schedule an appointment with yourself, 15-20 minutes to devote to conscious worrying. Keeping it to that timespan can free up your mind and not take over the whole day (Morin, 2018).

9. Bridges: Marvelous Structures of Transition

As a driver, I take bridges for granted. Yet, what a phenomenal engineering feat to be able to cross something—a river, a canyon, or a lake—in a car. How engineers design these incredible structures is beyond my realm of comprehension. The precision with which they are planned and constructed from start to finish must take considerable intelligence, attention to detail, and teamwork. From the Golden Gate Bridge to the Brooklyn Bridge to the London Bridge and bridges all over the world, these connectors represent magnificent feats.

Perhaps my admiration for bridges reflects my growing up next to a bridge that crossed the Allegheny River. The bridge was the connector between our neighborhood and the rest of the town. Once, when the river flooded, our neighborhood was cut off. The bridge withstood the flood, but there was no way to access it.

In life, bridges can represent connectors, but a better word may be "transitions." They help us to move from one thing to another. Structural bridges allow us to drive over something in a fairly seamless manner. However, bridges in life may not be as smooth. Bridges through grief can certainly have some dips along the way. Bridges through transition—moving to a new place, for example—can include some sharp turns. Bridges through life stages may also be rife with challenges. For instance, the bridge from adolescence to young adulthood can be filled with questions, changing expectations, and challenges not yet faced.

Final Tune-Up: Life's bridges may not be paved smoothly, but they can surely help a person to successfully traverse difficult times.

Questions for Driving Your Life:

1. Have you experienced anxiety crossing a bridge in your life or a fear of what waits on the other side?

2. Are you currently on a bridge in life? If so, how far along the bridge are you?

3. Pretend for a moment that you are an engineer who builds life bridges. How would you design them? What would be the details in the bridge that make it uniquely designed by you?

Fuel for thought: Acknowledging a birthday is a bridge from one year to the next. Celebrating birthdays has steadily become a worldwide practice as each birthday brings hope of another year. The modern-day cake that often accompanies this passage came about in the late 18th century in Germany. It was there that they commemorated *Kinderfeste*, a celebration for children that included a candle for each year alive—and one for the next—as well as making a wish when blowing them out (Van Luling, 2017).

10. Engine Lights: Breakdown in Utica

It was an overcast Monday morning in Boston as I headed west on the Massachusetts Turnpike. About halfway across the state, my red "check engine" light came on. If that has happened to you, you know it causes a sinking feeling, to be sure. All kinds of thoughts immediately start: *Oh, no, this could be a big problem. What should I do? Where is the nearest garage?* I was in the midst of a nine-hour drive and certainly didn't feel like stopping. After all, the car was running fine. How serious could it be?

I made it to Albany where I was meeting a friend for lunch. His advice? Keep going and have it checked out when I got home. That certainly sounded good to me, and so I continued on my merry way. About 90 minutes later, while going 60 mph on the New York State Thruway, my car suddenly died. It was towed to a garage, where I was told they couldn't fix it until the next day. Upon my first visit to Utica, I found a hotel, waited for the rather expensive repair (timing belt), and departed the next day. And that's how I learned the lesson to listen to the wisdom of that tiny light on my dashboard. "Check engine" lights are bright red for a reason and are not something to be ignored

As easy as it was for me to dismiss the information from my car's warning system, our own defense mechanisms in life make it seem (at the time) easier to ignore a problem instead of facing it. Our rationalization tells us that the situation is no big deal and certainly not a serious concern. Our denial may even say that there is no problem and that perhaps the indicator itself is simply broken or in error.

Avoidance (procrastination) may also enter the picture, with the approach of deciding to take care of it tomorrow, then the next day, and the day after. Sooner or later, however, the warning can have negative consequences.

Final Tune-Up: Be mindful of life's "check engine lights," as they are there for a reason.

Questions for Driving Your Life:

1. What are some "check engine" lights that have surfaced in your life?

2. What have been the consequences for not heeding the light (sooner than later)?

3. If you were to design some "check engine lights" for your life, what would they be and what would they be telling you to watch out for?

Fuel for thought: Small doses of stress can give you the motivation to accomplish something in the moment. However, the body can give off numerous warning indicators in the form of emotions and physical signs when feeling stress for too long, akin to a "check engine" light. Paying attention to the body's signals can help an individual manage stress more effectively and reduce its long-term impact on health (American Psychological Association, 2008).

11. Mountains and Tunnels: How Do You Relate to Challenges?

Terrains aren't all flat, so engineers and construction workers making roadways encounter all types of challenging landscapes in their work. The path plan sometimes leads right up to a mountain. What to do? Go around, through, or over it? Those tasked with completing the roadway must consider all types of variables, including costs, the height of the mountain, and the surrounding environment.

One way to allow car travel in a mountainous area is to create a tunnel, a hole in the mountain for vehicles to pass through. It's a brilliant solution, though not an easy one. Drilling horizontally through the earth, especially when it's rocky, must be tremendously difficult.

Drilling a good roadway tunnel takes precision. It is also done mostly in the dark. Seeing the light at the end of the tunnel must come as a welcome relief!

Life's problems can be seen the same way: Mountains get in the way of what we want. What do we do about these mountains? Pretending that they aren't there in the first place is called *denial*. Finding a way to go way around them is called *avoidance*. Then there is a direct approach: the tunnel (which is not always the right approach to take).

The tunnel approach to life can be scary because of the darkness, the uncertainty of the process, and not knowing how long that it will take to complete the tunnel. However, seeing that dim light toward the end of the tunnel can bring tremendous joy in realizing the goal has nearly been accomplished.

Final Tune-Up: Tunneling through life's problems requires facing challenges directly. A tunnel offers a direct and oftentimes more effective route to travel. Might the same hold true for some problems in life?

Questions for Driving Your Life:

1. What is your preferred route when it comes to obstacles?

2. What has been your experience in making a tunnel through a life mountain?

3. What advice would you give a best friend about making such a tunnel?

Fuel for thought: When it comes to facing obstacles, hopeful people are more likely to find a way around them, be more flexible in their thinking, and be uplifted by support systems that are drawn to their upbeat and optimistic natures (Snyder, Rand, & Sigmon, 2002).

12. Glove Compartment: What is in Yours?

The *glove compartment* or *glove box*, whatever you call this tucked-away area of your car, it's a wonderfully handy part of the front seat area. Not many people these days utilize it to hold gloves, but it's remarkably useful. It can hold numerous small items, and can even be locked.

Now think for a moment: Would you be able to tell me what is in your glove compartment? I bet you could tell me some things, but not others. Many people keep their automobile registration, insurance, and vehicle manual there, all of which are necessary to have in critical times. If you peeked in mine, you'd also find assorted paper, pens (some that might even work), and who knows what else.

The glove compartment has fascinating origins, and it may be one of the few features that remain from the first automobiles. The 1900 Packard offered drivers a glove compartment because many cars didn't have roofs at that time. As a result, many drivers wore gloves, and what better place to store them than the "glove compartment," which became standard in most cars by the 1930s (Adams, 2007). It is easy to see how this feature would "add value" to a car owner. Can you imagine how having a "glove compartment" in one's life could add value?

Final Tune-Up: Life's treasures need to be valued and kept close to you.

Questions for Driving Your Life:

1. Congratulations! You have a new car. (Don't you love that scent?) What will you put into the empty glove compartment?

2. But wait a moment: Before driving away in the new car, you have to clean out the glove compartment of your old car. What is in there? Is there anything worth keeping? If so, what are those items?

3. At what times in life does your glove compartment need to be locked?

Fuel for thought: What do the treasures that you keep in your glove compartment say about you? In New Zealand, for example, early childhood educators collaborated with researchers on ways to strengthen the identity of children of immigrant and refugee families. A "treasure box" component was a part of the project, as students used artifacts from their homelands to develop cultural ties and relationships with peers (Treweek, 2020).

13. The Exhaust Pipe: Can't Live Without It!

Everyone who knows me well knows that I am far from mechanical. I have little knowledge of how a car operates. I imagine a car as a body, a lot of parts working simultaneously, with the oil representing the body's blood keeping the motor (heart) running. Simple, I know.

Then there is the exhaust system. If the engine generates energy (if you're an engineer, I can see you wincing), then there has to be a certain amount of waste. I recall walking underneath my car while it was elevated at the muffler shop and thinking, *Wow, there's a lot more under here than I ever expected.* If one part of the exhaust system goes awry, the odor is enough to tell any driver that something needs to be repaired.

Similarly, life has its own "exhaust system." We leave things behind, we lose things, and sometimes we are the one left behind by another. Some of these losses are natural, as in leaving childhood behind in reaching adulthood. In other instances, they are purposeful, as in choosing to follow another religious faith, leave your hometown, or to change jobs.

I recall an interesting quote, the author of which I can't remember: "Some things lost are not worth keeping." As someone who often misplaces things, this quote comes to mind often. Yet the point is intriguing: We do spend time looking for lost items—and sometimes lost people—only to find that they weren't worth finding after all.

Final Tune-Up: Losses occur. They are an inherent part of life.

Questions for Driving Your Life:

1. Was there ever a point in your life when you spent an abundance of time looking for a lost item, only to truly wonder if it was worth the effort?

2. How do you cope with loss?

3. How would you realize that your life's exhaust system needed to be replaced?

Fuel for thought: If you are trying to decide if it is time to let something go, Cameroonian writer Kamga Tchassa (2019) suggests that one sign is being able to imagine the future without the thing, person, or situation.

18

PART 2

Preparation

Maintenance

14. Energy: What Kind Do You Use?

It used to be more straightforward and you could ask, "What kind of gasoline do you use?" With the advent of hybrid and electric cars, gasoline is no longer the only option. However, all cars need some kind of energy to move. Ever run out of gas or an electric charge? No fun at all. The car is working fine, but has no fuel on which to run.

The energy you choose to power your car may come down to costs, car maintenance, or your car itself. Whatever you select, something is needed if you expect to use your car to go to work, shopping, or on a vacation.

In a similar vein, each of us needs energy to function properly. The food that you eat may depend on preferences, cost, allergies, or what is available where you live. If you're similar to me, a diet of chocolate sounds pretty good, but probably isn't the most nutritious "fuel" for staying healthy.

In American society, an emphasis on diet and weight loss permeates the media. You may hear similar messages from your doctor during an annual physical, where getting a "clean bill of health" is about mental and physical health, fitness, and well-being—much of which is determined by the foods we eat. Your body needs fuel, to be sure, but it's up to you to choose the best fuel for your health and well-being.

Final Tune-Up: High-quality gasoline is preferred by some drivers because they believe it can help their car run more efficiently. The same applics to food and your body.

Questions for Driving Your Life:

1. Do you put premium gasoline in your car, but put unhealthy foods into your body?

2. Cars have alternative energy options. What alternative sources of energy do you consume?

3. If you could eat differently, what differences would you make?

Fuel for Thought: In a study at Cornell University, it was found that the size of plates and bowls had a significant influence on how hungry a person felt. The study found that people make at least 200 decisions concerning food on a daily basis, but may be as much as 90 percent unaware of these choices and how they are affected by food cues in their environment (Wansink, 2007).

15. Cars are Complicated: And So are You!

This title is meant as a compliment. Let me explain: I was 17 years old and riding in the back seat of a car driven by my friend's father. It was a Friday night, and some friends and I were headed to an out-of-town high school football game. In the midst of our conversation, the father said, "It's a wonder that cars move as well as they do. Do you realize the belts in this engine are rotating hundreds of time a minute?"

That moment and comment stayed with me. So much is happening under the hood each time you turn on the ignition and press the accelerator. Between the ignition system, the cooling system, the exhaust system, and the many belts all working in conjunction, the car to me is a mechanical marvel. It takes all of them—and much more—working properly to ensure the car functions reliably to get us from here to there.

In a similar vein, it certainly takes a great deal for you to "run." Think about the intricate systems in your own body—immune, respiratory, and circulatory, to name a few—and how imperative they are to your mental and physical health. Likewise, consider the other systems in your life: your family system, your community, your intrapersonal system, and your support system. A disruption in one of them can lead to a disruption in your own functioning.

Just as your car needs a tune-up to check its various systems, we can use the same thing. I mentioned an annual physical exam in #18, but when it comes to mental health and well-being, counseling can be a great help to people. Whether a handful of sessions or a longer-term process, talking to a mental health professional can be a useful tune-up for your level of life contentment and wellness.

Final Tune-Up: Counseling = life tune-up. It is worth considering (since maintenance can prevent breakdowns).

Questions for Driving Your Life:

1. Examine the functioning of your own life systems. How are they doing?

2. Do you see counseling as a sign of weakness or a tune-up? Has your opinion changed?

3. If you were to seek counseling, what do you think would be helpful to talk about?

Fuel for Thought: Some ways that talk therapy can be of benefit is having the chance to tell your story, identifying patterns in behaviors, normalizing problems by knowing others go through similar things, getting tools to change your life, and the offering of hope that things can improve (Lloyd, 2010).

16. Supercars: Should Cars be Exercised?

"Supercars?"

Not to worry…I hadn't heard the word before, either. After reading Motavalli's (2020) article, I discovered that they are the Lamborghinis and Ferraris of the road—high-luxury, expensive cars that can go fast. Really, really fast.

Take a moment and think about the last time that you saw a supercar whizzing past you on the interstate or even cruising by your house. Maybe neither has ever happened. After all, those cars are seen in action movies, but not often in real life.

Many supercars aren't driven. They look new, but aren't. Motavalli (2020) described a 1990 Lamborghini—a car capable of speeds of 190 mph—that had only 83 miles on its odometer. According to Motavalli, "the car has almost never moved under its own power." If Interested in buying it, the sales price is merely $622,000. Another 1990 Lamborghini at the same dealership—this one with 11,000 miles on it—had an asking price of $335,000. Meanwhile, a 1991 Ferrari with 1,705 miles was purchased for about $1.7 million in 2019.

Imagine owning a car, an expensive car at that, yet not driving it. Jay Leno, the famed comedian who collects cars, takes a different tact in saying, "Cars are like people—they need to be exercised" (as cited in Motavalli, 2020).

Perhaps Leno's point applies to our physical wellness. We can do our utmost to practice other forms of wellness, such as a nutritious diet and proper sleep habits, but that *movement* part is critical. Inactivity kills more people than smoking, and sitting six or more hours a day heightens the risk of an early death (Rath, 2013). Just two hours on your rear end lowers good cholesterol by 20 percent. Altogether, as Rath pointed out, "Sitting is the most underrated health threat of modern times" (p. 21).

Undriven supercars are also at risk. Car collector James Glickenhaus outlines the perils of ruined carburetors, hardened brake fluid, clogged radiators, and corrosive-releasing oil in trying to preserve low-mileage supercars (Motavalli, 2020).

Final Tune-Up: Treating our bodies like collectible supercars is most likely not the answer.

Questions for Driving Your Life:

1. How much time do you spend sitting? How much of a threat is that in your life?

2. Have you ever experienced the equivalent of a ruined carburetor or clogged radiators from inactivity?

3. What might be some simple ways to be even a little more active?

Fuel for Thought: If risks haven't happened to us or someone we know, we might discard important information as irrelevant. That was the message from one psychologist, Dr. Sara Boilen, who also happens to be an avalanche educator in Montana. "If I've skied 100 days in the backcountry, I've never had an avalanche, and I've never had to dig my friend out, my brain has effectively disposed of all the information I have about how to shovel out from an avalanche," she said (Maltarich, 2021).

Social Support

17. Pit Crews: Who is in Your Support Group?

Imagine being a NASCAR driver for a moment. Going around the track multiple times at 100 to 200 miles per hour, having to watch several cars around you going the same speed, being mindful of weather and track conditions, and communicating with the crew chief, all at the same time. It must be incredibly stressful. Oh, yes, and there is the race car, a finely tuned machine that is forced to withstand tremendous pressure for hours.

With the possibilities of sparkplugs going bad, a tire blowing out, and a myriad of malfunctions in between, the pit crew of mechanics must be ready for anything at a moment's notice. The key ingredients in such a crew must be teamwork that features precision, communication, and expertise. Put these together and one asset surfaces: support.

Without a good crew team, the drivers—as skilled as they may be—would be helpless. Could you imagine if drivers had to pull into a pit and fix the cars themselves? The race would take so long and become so boring that spectators would head for the exits.

Think for a moment about the importance of having your own pit crew in life, a team of supporters cheering you on from the sidelines, offering advice and comfort, and simply being there for you when you need a pit stop. What a wonderful thing it is to have a crew team! Just like a race car driver who tries to fix their own car, trying to fix all your own problems will *not* work. Do you know someone in life who is self-reliant to the point of being unhealthy? They either don't have or, rather sadly, don't think they need a crew team.

Final Tune-Up: Having support in life can be healthy, smart, and enjoyable.

1. How would you describe the crew team in your life?

2. If you wanted to improve your crew team, where would you start?

3. How would you describe a person without a crew team in their life? Has that person ever been you?

Fuel for Thought: Research analyzing 148 studies with more than 300,000 subjects suggested that individuals with social support, including contact with family, friends and the community, were 50% more likely to live 3.7 years longer than people with fewer connections. It was also found that individuals lacking in social support experienced mortality risks equal to alcoholism and greater than obesity and physical inactivity (Dayton, 2010).

18. AAA: Breakdown, Anyone?

On a brisk fall morning in 2001, I received an early morning phone call from my wife. On her way to work, her car had blown a tire. I bundled up our 11-month-old daughter and drove to my wife's disabled car. She proceeded to work in the car that worked, while my daughter and I waited for close to two hours for roadside assistance. We spent the time walking up and down the street, admiring leaves and trees and anything else that caught our attention.

I recall the morning with great detail, as it was the 11th of September in 2001. Unbeknownst to me and my daughter, unspeakable tragedies were happening in the country while we waited for help for a 1998 Toyota RAV-4 with one bad tire, which, in retrospect, seemed so inconsequential.

Bad and sometimes horrific things happen in life, such as abuse, death, tragedy, a breakup, cancer, or other illness. These trials bring a great deal of stress that can take their toll on us physically, mentally, and interpersonally. In these hard times, an emotional pick-me-up can truly come in handy and sometimes be a lifesaver.

Just as AAA comes to offer emergency roadside assistance, it is comforting to have a "triple-A" in your life. To whom can you turn in times of despair, heartache, and grief? Who represents your 24/7 support, available to you at any time of the day or night to provide comfort or lend an ear? Everyone needs a help-on-call person in life, but sadly, some don't have anyone to fill that role.

Remember the two major tenets of Reality Therapy: One of the basic and most primary of human needs is to love and to belong, and people need satisfying relationships in their lives to help fulfill their needs. The theory also espouses the concept of the quality world, which includes the specific people who help to fulfill needs. Some people try to drive their lives with a sparse, if not completely empty, world where satisfying relationships don't exist (Corey, 2013).

<u>Final Tune-Up</u>: Supportive people in times of need can make a significant difference.

<u>Questions for Driving Your Life</u>:

1. Who can you call when you need "roadside assistance" in life?

2. Would you like to have more people in your world?

3. If so, how do you see yourself building additional satisfying relationships in life?

<u>Fuel for Thought</u>: Do you have trouble asking for help? Suggestions include making a list of what kind of help you may need; listing names of friends or family who have offered to help recently or in the past; matching individuals with tasks that reflect their interests, strengths, availability, and abilities; and being direct and to the point of asking for what you need to avoid waiting for others to offer (Bernhard, 2011).

19. Tailgating: The Car Party Manifested

What comes to mind when you think of "tailgating?" Likely, a sporting event like football, coupled with the smell of grilled burgers, various beverages, seeing old friends, and a general party atmosphere revolving around a favorite sports team.

Pick-up trucks and SUVs with actual tailgates are prevalent at these social events, but any vehicle will do—especially if it's decorated. I've seen huge RVs in a football stadium parking lot that are so colorfully branded you would think they were the team bus. The parking lot parties at concerts can also be remarkable. Jimmy Buffet fans in particular are famous for "Parrothead" themed cars, trucks, buses, and trailers with Buffet fans congregating all day long before a concert.

And, there is far more to these parked-car communities than meets the eye. According to John Sherry, a researcher at the University of Notre Dame, a tailgate party represents a microcosm of society with its own neighborhoods, traditions, inter-generational communities, and team brands (Carter, 2012). Sherry noted that some tailgaters have gathered in the same location for years. One story from the pre-game festivities at the University of Utah revealed two couples who met across the tailgating "street." One of them ended up organizing a wedding shower for the other and attended the funeral when a relative passed away (Carter). As a member of one of the couples said, "If they're wearing a Utah shirt, you'll give them anything."

Food, furniture, games, family mementos…and fun. Cars bring a sense of community and belonging. It really is more complicated that one might realize. Sherry described the college tailgating adventure as "a very complex social, community-building exercise…[in] which fans are able to connect with and actually help create their school's brand" (Chapla, 2012).

According to something called "choice theory," people are born with five basic needs, the most primary of which is "love and belonging" (Corey, 2017). Maybe, just maybe, these parked-car parties are fulfilling this need prior to soccer matches, football games, and concerts. For some, the attitude is: who cares about the actual event? Albright (2014) cited a study that found as many as 35% of tailgaters never even stepped foot inside the stadium!

Final Tune-Up: Vehicles can facilitate gatherings and provide social benefits.

Questions for Driving Your Life:

1. Observe your next—possibly your first—tailgating experience. What do you notice in regard to team branding, social interactions, and community building?

2.   What are everyday ways in which cars can help people find some sense of belonging?

3.   In what new, innovative ways can cars be used to draw people together in community spirit?

Fuel for Thought: Without events like tailgating parties to turn to, some people need to be more proactive about socializing. In a collective living experiment in Sweden, 72 people living in an apartment building signed a contract promising to spend at least two hours per week with each other. Half of the residents were under 25; the other half were in older adulthood. One of the managers described the goal in saying, "We try to work against loneliness, to make people be more socially included" (Savage, 2020).

20. Teaching Someone to Drive: The Manual of Life

I could live until the ripe young age of 100 and still remember the name of my driver's education teacher: Mr. Jim Lucco. In the summer of 1978, he had the patience and bravery to teach me and my high school classmates the art and science of driving.

I ask this question: How many people would want to be a driver's education teacher for 17-year-olds who have minimal driving experience? I know I wouldn't be the first to volunteer.

Yet Mr. Lucco did…and I will always remember the calmness he brought to the passenger seat at 8:30 am (quite early for many teens) on weekdays in July. He spoke slowly; he spoke with encouragement; he spoke with a conviction that we could indeed learn this petrifying act of exceeding my previous top speed of 12 mph on a bike.

Who has been in your passenger seat of life? What roles have they taken—navigator, agitator, or fellow human being along for the ride and a good conversation?

If you went through the songs on my workout playlist, you'd find "Movin' Right Along," a wonderful song (Ascher & Williams, 1979) delivered by Kermit the Frog and Fozzie Bear of Muppet fame. I never tire of this duet from *The Muppet Movie*, as the pair sets off in their cross-country trek by car to Hollywood. "With good friends, you can't lose," in adventures and in life.

Final Tune-Up: Who is in your passenger seat?

Questions for Driving Your Life:

1. In your current stretch on your road of life, what kind of person do you need in your passenger seat: a guide, a teacher, a listener, or a coach?

2. Are you currently in the passenger seat of someone else's life? If so, how are you being helpful in their drive?

3. Mr. Lucco spoke calmly, with encouragement and conviction. What qualities would you bring to the passenger seat…and how can those same qualities help when *you* are in the driver's seat?

Fuel for Thought: How important is it to help others in their drive of life? Burns, Sholtis, Lemmer, Rauk, and Mohamed (2020) asked licensed counselors about the values they brought to their work. Perhaps, not surprisingly, over three-quarters of them (80%) expressed the value of helping others to find their potential. One participant wrote, "When I help a person reach their full potential, I am impacting the whole of our society" (p. 243).

Communication

21. Signs: They Are All Around Us

As the youngest of eight children, I grew up listening to the music of my older siblings. I recall a song called "Signs" by the Five Man Electric Band, which mentions signs being everywhere. How true!

Signs surround us as drivers, instructing us to yield, stop, where to park, and how fast to drive. These signs inform, warn, and direct us. Without them, we would get lost, get into an accident, or create chaos on the roadways.

And so it is with life and its road markers. Has anyone ever yelled, "C'mon, can't you read the sign?" as if you weren't supposed to miss it? However, as we drive, our focus can be elsewhere, making us oblivious to signs, large and small.

Sometimes overt and other times more subtle, life also has signs. Some are described as "mental clocks" (Neugarten, 1979) which people use to determine whether they are "on time" in regard to things like marriage, parenthood, and retirement (pp.888-889). There can be external pressure to adhere to the signs, such as a nagging parent continually asking her newlywed son or daughter, "Isn't it time that you had a baby?"

Sometimes dates are signs. In the US, for example, April 15th is for many a large, brightly-colored, flashing sign on the calendar that cannot be ignored (taxes aren't optional). Birthdays can also be a sign. Turning 40 or 50? Some birthdays seem to be more significant mile markers than others.

For some, anniversaries can be signs of celebration (wedding) or grieving (death). These same signs can be markers, as can any date of personal significance. For instance, Boxing Day (December 26) is a special day in Ireland. According to family folklore, an ancestor of ours declared that their family—and subsequent generations—would not eat meat on Boxing Day if they survived the potato famine.

Remember, too, that signs don't have to stay the same. I recently drove by a fast food restaurant and saw an employee changing the message on the outdoor sign. Interested in changing the content of your sign?

<u>Final Tune-Up</u>: Signs in life are evident in various ways.

<u>Questions for Driving Your Life</u>:

1. Has anyone ever scolded you for not reading a sign in life? What was your response?

2. What sign do you need to see in your life right now? What would it look like?

3. What important signs have been part of your past? What important signs are up ahead in your future?

<u>Fuel for Thought</u>: Sometimes the signs that are flashing brightest for us to notice are the ones pointing out what we haven't finished. The unconscious mind might be trying to get our attention by making us think more about unfinished tasks than about accomplishments. This is known as the *Zeigarnik effect* and may be a source of increased stress and anxiety if one tries to suppress thoughts about incomplete tasks (Vinney, 2019).

22. Turn Signals: It's About Communication

I am fascinated by turn signals and would like to meet the person who created them. Simple, yet ingenious, indeed. They are a wonderful way to communicate with another person (driver, cyclist, or pedestrian) by virtue of simply shifting a lever. Without them, driving would be quite a different experience. Imagine the chaos of drivers yelling out their car windows, "Attention, everyone! I'm turning left at this intersection!"

To get to the neighborhood where I lived as a boy, one had to cross a bridge. Whenever I was riding with my father, he would automatically put on the car's turn signal indicator as we approached the turn for the bridge. One day my brother asked, "Dad, why do you turn on your turn signal so early?" My father's answer was clear: "Better too early than too late."

Ever drive behind someone who didn't use a turn signal? No doubt that has happened to us all. How frustrating was that for you? There may have been a close call, or worse yet, an accident, when that other driver made an unexpected turn.

And so it is with life's turn signals, which reflect clear, direct communication about what a person is going to do. This is especially valuable in the workforce and in interpersonal relationships. Just as a turn signal shows the intent of direction, people's clear expressions show healthy communication.

Final Tune-Up: Healthy communication—the turn signals of life—is a vital ingredient for healthy relationships.

Questions for Driving Your Life:

1. How are you using your turn signals in life?
2. What is it like to be around someone who doesn't use turn signals? Have you ever been that type of person?
3. Is your turn signal weak or broken? How can you fix it?

Fuel for Thought: It is all too easy for miscommunication to occur. Ernest Hemingway reportedly said, "Most people never listen" (as cited in Marino, 2019, para 1).

23. Backseat Drivers: Who Needs Them?

Have you ever had the experience of driving with a passenger who told you how to drive with every little turn? Not too pleasant, is it? In fact, it can be annoying, stressful, and downright insulting.

Life can have its share of backseat drivers, those individuals who frequently tell you what to do and how to do it. And they do so without being asked. Their remarks are often critical and usually involve the word *should*. "You should drive slower." "You shouldn't be so reckless." "It shouldn't be taking this long to find our way there."

What is it like to frequently be told what to do and how to act without having a voice of your own? You may want to tell someone, "Hey, I can do this myself, thank you very much," but tuning out a back seat driver can be tough. It's important to remember that a back seat driver wants the same thing we want: to get to the destination safely. Life's back seat drivers also want good outcomes for us. Understanding that is the first step; reframing their messages is the second step.

Now change the scenario: What would it be like to have a complimentary back seat driver who reinforces your efforts and honors the difficulties encountered behind the wheel? How soothing it would be, as a driver, to hear: "You've really handled the driving duties so well," or "You were able to stay so focused while driving through that rainstorm." No doubt this would be a pleasant scenario.

Final Tune-Up: Critical as they may seem, back seat drivers really do care and want good outcomes for us drivers. What an opportunity to reframe their comments!

Questions for Driving Your Life:

1. How do you cope with the back seat drivers in life?

2. Have you yourself ever been a back seat driver?

3. What would it be like to morph into a positive back seat driver?

Fuel for Thought: Researchers have found that turning negative thinking into helpful messages can improve confidence. Unfortunately, the brain's response is minimal since it tends to respond more quickly to negative thoughts and words—due to them signaling a possible threat to survival (Waldman & Newber, 2012).

24. Hitchhiking: It Was All About One Thing

Ever since the passing of horse-and-buggy days, without owning a car, truck, or motorcycle, it can be difficult to get around. Yes, there are bikes, subways, and buses, but some destinations are difficult to reach using those modes of transportation. Not that many years ago, people often hitchhiked from place to place. Many years ago my brother picked up a hitchhiker who ended up in the NBA Hall of Fame! (At 6'11", I wonder how he even got into my brother's car.)

My own personal hitchhiking story taught me a useful lesson. After working in Dublin for some time in the mid-1980s, I decided it was time for me to see the rest of Ireland. On a rainy Saturday morning, I took a bus to the southern outskirts of the city with my bright orange backpack, stuck out my thumb, and proceeded to watch hundreds, if not thousands, of cars pass me by. About an hour later, a car finally stopped. I climbed aboard and struck up a conversation with an architect who not only took me to a famous church nearby, but also insisted that I stay with him for the weekend!

The following day I had to ask my new friend, "What prompted you to pick me up?"

"Oh, it's simple, John," he said. "When I drove by you, you looked me in the eye. That said a lot." Eye contact has cultural ramifications to be sure, and in this case, it certainly paid off for me.

Though I don't advocate hitchhiking these days, my experience was a telling one that I draw on when interacting with others. It can certainly apply to counseling, too.

Final Tune-Up: Making eye contact with others can have a profound impact on your personal and professional life.

Questions for Driving Your Life:

1. How is it perceived when you make eye contact with someone in the cultures to which you belong?

2. How do you see other people?

3. How do you view another person who fails to look at you when speaking?

Fuel for Thought: Eye contact plays a key role in what psychologists refer to as *resonance*, an automatic and often unconscious process that takes cues from eye contact and facial expressions, enhancing social connection, love and empathy (Seppala, 2012).

Rejuvenation

25. Rest Stops: Not the Best Name, But a Wonderful Idea

You are driving on the interstate highway and pass a sign that says, "NEXT REST STOP- 11 MILES." The stop may have several restaurants or a simple vending machine. It may have nice restroom facilities or a portable toilet. They truly range, but the point is that they offer drivers and passengers an opportunity to stop and take a break.

I used to be the type of person who was anti-rest stop. I would see the sign for the next stop and often think, "Oh, I can make it to the stop *after* that." Then, as I came upon that next pull-off, I would think the same thing. Yes, my stomach might have been growling. Yes, my body was yearning for a bathroom break, but I still thought I didn't *have* to stop. In my mind, getting to the destination was more important. Rest stops! Who needs them?

In life, everyone needs them. Rest stops help us to slow down, to take care of our needs, and exit the highway of life. Re-nourishment and refreshment are certainly necessary and good for our well-being.

Final Tune-Up: Sometimes life wants us to stop, but we don't. Rest is critical.

Questions for Driving Your Life:

1. When was the last time you used a rest stop?

2. Who or what represents a rest stop in your life?

3. If you haven't been stopping to rest in your life, when and where can you create even one rest stop?

Fuel for Thought: Your brain needs rest, too. It seems the brain is more wired to respond to change rather than focusing on one thing for

37

a long time, so short breaks of stopping and starting again can serve one better to enhance focus and creativity (Ariga & Lleras, 2011).

26. Red Lights: Invitations to Pause

Other countries may have a running of the bulls, but the US has something every day: the running of the red lights. When a light turns yellow, you know that the red light is on the way, yet for many, that signal means hitting the accelerator. I once took a city tour of Kansas City and the guide said something like, "In our town, green means go, red means stop, and yellow means that at least eight more cars are going to try to make it through."

In our society, going is better than stopping, proceeding is better than waiting, and moving is better than sitting. There's a definite tendency to rush. Just look at the expression, to *run* a red light.

Let's look at this a different way. Consider the notion that getting a red light is actually a good thing. It forces us to stop, even if we don't want to do so. Slowing down, listening to music, and looking around the intersection can be pleasant diversions from our rush-rush world. Stop lights are the road's way of saying, "Chill out and enjoy the ride! No need to hurry." Instead of seeing a red light with anger, think of it as a soothing, caring message—like a red heart.

In life, stop light times are when we have the chance to relax, slow down and be calm. In England, tea time can serve this purpose. Meditation, yoga, and jogging can be stop lights. Sketching or playing music can be a stop light.

Go ahead, enjoy a red light in life today.

Final Tune-Up: Red light = Relaxation.

Questions for Driving Your Life:

1. What is your favorite color in a traffic light? Your least favorite?

2. Do you have life red lights? If not, what would they be?

3. What would your life be like if you enjoyed red lights every day?

<u>Fuel for Thought</u>: Red lights may stop drivers, but they don't always calm us. The concept of *traffic calming* was first developed in Europe to enhance safety for motorists and spaces for pedestrians as well as improving the quality of traffic environments. *Traffic calming* techniques can slow the pace of vehicles and serve to calm drivers or walkers with well-placed painted lines, colors, patterns, traffic circles, road humps, or planters (Project for Public Spaces, 2008).

27. Interstates vs. Back Roads: What is Your Pace?

Imagining life without interstate highways is like imagining life without computers. Think about a time in the US when no interstate highways existed. There were only two-lane roads, if that! Driving 200 miles was considered a major trip and took much more time than we would expect today. (At least the gasoline was inexpensive.)

When interstate highways were built, they helped drivers in many ways. Why use the old two-lane road when you could drive at faster speeds, avoid bends and washouts in the road, and not have to be concerned about traffic lights? On top of it all, you could get to your destination much more quickly. It may take 40 minutes to get to a nearby town on the local highway, but taking the interstate could get you there in half the time.

The interstate reflects a value in American society: speed. We like things to be *fast*. We want drive-through restaurants, banks, and pharmacies. We want instant access to information on our cellphones. We want direct flights instead of having a layover somewhere.

Speediness has its value in life; there's no doubting that. However, speed and hurry can also induce stress, a frequent by-product of the emphasis on quickness. The old local two-lane highway allows for a more pleasant pace, a quieter, calmer drive, and often a more scenic one. There is something to be said for that road and that pace.

<u>Final Tune-Up</u>: While speed in life is often valued, consider the advantages of just slowing down.

<u>Questions for Driving Your Life</u>:

1. Answer the following without giving it a second thought. Interstate or two-lane road: Which do you prefer? Why?

2. Do you find that stress creeps in when you hurry in life?

3. Opt to take a local highway (or "back road") on your next commute or journey. How is it different for you?

Fuel for Thought: Giving your brain a chance to slow down and experience some downtime can allow it the opportunity to incorporate new learning, replay conversations, or engage in self-reflection. Epiphanies, those profound realizations that seem to come out of the blue, may occur due to mental downtime allowing unconscious activity to reach the surface (Jabr, 2013).

28. Garages: A Place of Rest

If you're fortunate enough to have a garage, you know how wonderful it can be, particularly when it is attached to your home and has an automatic door. To be able to park your car, close the garage door, and go into your home on a rainy afternoon or a snowy evening can be a welcome relief from the elements. It's also a home for your car, a safe place. If the day arrives when cars can talk, I wonder what they would say upon arriving in the garage after a 13-hour return trip from your relative's home. My guess? "Whew! Glad to be home."

The same applies to life when it comes to sleep and rest. About a third of American adults say that their sleep levels don't meet the recommended levels, which is one reason why caffeinated, energy-boosting drinks are used as frequently as they are. Moreover, a lack of sleep can be connected to a number of diseases and medical conditions, including diabetes, cardiovascular disease, depression, and obesity (Centers for Disease Control and Prevention, 2020a). Driving while drowsy can also be and is related to a number of accidents, injuries, and deaths (Centers for Disease Control and Prevention, 2020b).

Garages are often cluttered with lots of stuff (okay, call it junk) that is really not needed, which prompts the eventual "garage sale." In some cases, people put so much stuff in their garages that they cannot even fit their car!

The same can also be said in situations where people clutter their lives with items, tasks, and relationships that don't have a truly meaningful place.

<u>Final Tune-Up</u>: A person's life garage should be a comfortable place.

<u>Questions for Driving Your Life</u>:

1.   What is in your life garage? How useful or helpful are the items that are there?

2.   Is there room for *you* in your life garage?

3.   What changes would you like to make in your life garage?

<u>Fuel for Thought</u>: Individuals who adopt a minimalist approach to living, such as those drawn to the "tiny house" lifestyle, report a greater sense of financial security, autonomy, greater meaning in relationships, enjoyment of the "simple life," and increased freedom to pursue life-enhancing activities (Mangold & Zschau, 2019).

Safety

29. Speed Limits: Ever Think About How They Protect You?

Speed limit signs. They are everywhere, though perhaps rarely noticed. Some people may detest them, seeing them as a "control" that limits how quickly they can drive. They may want to go faster—and may indeed do so (see #10!)—but the speed limit reflects the law. Ever been in a hurry and wanted to go faster, but didn't because of the speed limit?

But did you ever stop to think about the utility of speed limits and how they are a friend rather than a foe? Speed limits are designed for safety and to protect ourselves and others. Adjacent to my daughters' elementary school was a 15-.mph speed zone, enforced during school hours. Before having children, I would have likely grumbled to myself as I came upon a school zone. As a parent, however, I appreciate these controls.

Speed limits are contextual, too. While 15 mph may be appropriate near a school, 30 mph is acceptable for neighborhood roads, and the interstate highway allows for 65 mph or even 70 mph. What is acceptable behavior in one place isn't acceptable in another place. Could you picture yourself driving 15 mph on a traffic-free I-95 outside of New York City? Other drivers would be outraged!

In teaching some courses, I have asked college students if they have ever received a speeding ticket and whether the corresponding fine changed their behavior. Many indicate that it did, but only for a short period. Others say that it made them slow down, but only in the area where they received the ticket.

Final Tune-Up: Speed limits are positive and designed to help us, regardless of how inconvenient some might view them.

1. What would it be like to drive without speed limits?

2. How do you define your own personal speed limit?

3. Consider things that affect fixed and temporary speed limits: the terrain, the weather, construction, and the size of the road. What elements of life affect your speed limits?

Fuel for Thought: In 2020, the upper house of the German Parliament vetoed the idea of an 80-mph speed limit on the autobahn road system (Perlberg, 2020).

Slowing down certainly has its benefits. For example, according to DoSomething.org, it takes 20 minutes for your brain to recognize that your stomach is full. Perhaps taking your time while eating has its benefits after all ("11 Facts About," n.d.).

30. Emergency Brakes: The Last-Minute Stops

It was a 100-year-old Victorian-style house with plenty of room and situated partway up a rather steep hill. Shortly after we moved in, we invited a friend for a dinner to see our new place. It was a wonderful evening until, around 11:00 p.m., she went to drive home and couldn't find her car! Stolen? No. Rather, it was "mis-parked." Her car had slipped out of park, moved into neutral, and slid down the hill, unbeknownst to any of us. She found her car in my neighbor's front yard about six houses down. Had she used her emergency brake when parking her car? You guessed it—no.

A brake system that works "in case of emergency" can be a real lifesaver. And sometimes a "stop, just in time" is crucial to doing our best in the game of life. Ever had a temptation to do something that you knew was not healthy? Sneak an extra piece of chocolate cake? Gossip about a coworker? Post a hasty, angry reaction on social media or via email? Use an illicit drug? These are times to employ your life emergency brake.

Simply engaging this important tool can prevent us from doing things that could be harmful to ourselves and others. People can use all kinds of emergency brakes—calling a friend/sponsor, removing themselves from a situation, simply saying *no*, counting to ten, or saying a prayer. Whatever they are, these emergency brakes can save us from something that we may later regret.

Final Tune-Up: Some newer cars have an automatic braking feature. Installing something like this in our personal lives can have advantages.

Questions for Driving Your Life:

1. Consider a personal behavior which you find yourself repeating, even after deciding it is not in your best interest. Would it be helpful to have something to keep you from doing it?

2. Make a list of some possible emergency brakes for yourself. What surprised you in creating this list?

3. Talk to some people around you. What emergency brakes are successful for them?

Fuel for Thought: Reaching for a piece of chocolate you don't need? Your emergency brake could be simply setting a timer. Research shows that waiting 15 minutes can stifle a craving (Kita et al., 2012).

31. Traffic Lights: Give Garrett Morgan Credit

Garrett Morgan was a most brilliant inventor. Born 12 years after the end of Civil War, Morgan went to Cincinnati in his mid-teens to look for work. Although he only had an elementary-school education, he found employment as a handyperson before working as a mechanic on sewing machines. He went on to obtain a patent for an improved sewing machine before starting his own repair business.

In 1914, he secured another patent, this one for a breathing device that became a prototype for gas masks during World War I. The invention won him first prize in an international competition in New York City.

Morgan's work, however, was not done, despite facing discrimination and prejudice as a Black inventor and businessperson. In 1923, after observing a carriage accident in Cleveland, he developed a new kind of traffic signal that included a warning light signaling a stop to drivers. He achieved additional patents for his invention—the prototype for the modern three-way traffic signal—in the US, Britain, and Canada. Morgan later sold the rights to his signal to General Electric for $40,000 (Biography.com, 2021).

Morgan's thinking and problem-solving skills have saved countless lives over all these years. While some people may be annoyed by sitting at a red light, consider how impossible it would be for traffic to flow without his inventive spirit and astute observation skills.

<u>Final Tune-Up</u>: Red light. Yellow light. Green light. They tell when to stop, use caution, or proceed. Traffic lights are abundant on the roads and in life, where people can provide these safety signals, too.

<u>Questions for Driving Your Life</u>:

1.   Who are the traffic-light people in your life who have watched out for your safety?

2.   Some people ignore the yellow light of caution to get past an intersection, only to have an accident. Can you think of when you ignored a marker of caution in your life?

3.   Think about a current challenge in life, whether it be in work, relationships, or finances. What color best represents your intuition about how to proceed?

<u>Fuel for Thought</u>: According to Gray (2014), the first permanent traffic light in New York City was installed in 1920. It was a gift from a wealthy physician who designed the device with green signifying "stop," while white meant "go." The red, yellow, and green colors of traffic lights are now ubiquitous and are even part of daily language. Consider hearing a "green light" comment on approving or moving forward with an idea from a colleague or friend, while hesitation is marked by a "yellow light" remark.

32. Tailgating: Version Two

Language is fascinating in that the same word can have two different meanings. In a previous chapter, "tailgating" was synonymous with fun social get-togethers.

Here, that is not the case. According to Merriam-Webster (n.d.), "tailgating" as a verb means "to drive dangerously close behind another vehicle." The key word, of course, is *dangerously*. The Minnesota Department of Transportation (n.d.) noted that rear-end collisions were the cause of 28% of car accidents and about 4% of fatal accidents in 2005. Its "Stop Tailgating" pilot project aimed to educate drivers on keeping safe distances—a minimum of three seconds—and offered a clever way to measure the time. When the car ahead of you passes a landmark, such as a sign, start counting, "one-Minnesota, two-Minnesota, three-Minnesota." (So much for using "Mississippi" to count!)

To combat tailgating, the Japanese government also tried an educational campaign to alleviate this rising problem in Japan (Inoue, Hashioka, & Takeshita., 2020). The Japanese term for it, *aori-unten*, also includes situations where a driver intentionally passes another driver, moves into their lane, and deliberately slows down. In the past two years, arrests for tailgating have nearly doubled, as this is considered a serious offense that can cause undue stress or trauma for the victims of tailgaters (in addition to contributing to car accidents).

Keeping appropriate space between cars amounts to safety. As I write this chapter during a global pandemic, the corresponding measure is social distancing: keeping the six-foot recommended space from another person as a way to prevent the spread of COVID-19.

Yet the tailgating analogy can take another turn. "Don't get too close" is an unspoken message from one driver to another. The same holds with people and cultures: Don't intrude upon my personal space. The amount of that space varies, of course, depending on the relationship between the two people. Intimacy involves personal closeness, while strangers in non-pandemic times may require at least three feet (to feel comfortable).

Final Tune-Up: According to Drum (2020), the origin of "social distancing" is difficult to determine, though one of the earlier uses of the term dates to 2003 and the SARS epidemic. Regardless, the "don't-get-too-close" idea was commonplace during the heights of the COVID-19 epidemic.

<u>Questions for Driving Your Life</u>:

1. A driver tailgating you vs. a person invading your personal space…how are the two experiences similar or different for you?

2. Perhaps, as a driver, you have been in a hurry and tailgated another car. You impatiently want the other car to do something—drive faster or get out of the way—so that you can proceed. In life, there may be times when we want *someone* to do *something* before we can act. How do you approach this situation?

3. Consider the "three-Minnesota rule" in measuring distance from a car in front of you. How could this be used to give people around us proper space?

<u>Fuel for Thought</u>: Though tailgating may not be good, other forms of closeness can be beneficial. Futrelle (2020) called friends and family "a mighty elixir" toward happiness, adding that many studies suggested that friends are truly important (p. 55). And, with closeness in mind, what about hugs? Parker-Pope (2021) discussed the research behind the benefits of such close encounters, including decreased blood pressure and increased oxytocin levels.

PART 3

Change

Reframing

33. Location, Location, Location: Heard this Before?

You hear it all the time when selling a house. People want a desirable location, and that is a primary selling point. So what does this have to do with cars? I once was driving on a local turnpike and out of the corner of my eye, I spied a little house very close to this major interstate, standing on its own, completely separated from the other houses nearby.

Yet here's the beauty of it: On that particular street in that particular area, someone will buy that house when it goes on the market. Maybe not the first day, but someone will see that house, its attractive features, its charm, its *potential*, or its price, and buy it—even if it is next to a busy turnpike. It is the right fit for the right person.

In life everyone has talents, gifts, and, most of all, potential. It's easy to see this in the amazing 8-year-old virtuoso violinist who is performing at Carnegie Hall in New York, but what about the at-risk child of the same age growing up in a low-income area somewhere in the U.S.? Sometimes it takes special people to see the assets of other special people. Perhaps you were one of them, a youth of tremendous potential that went untapped until that one teacher, coach, or tutor saw your inner spark and encouraged you to grow. They made a difference, just as you can make a difference in others.

<u>Final Tune-Up</u>: Everyone has positive qualities that can be noticed by others.

<u>Questions for Driving Your Life</u>:

1. Can you relate to the seemingly lonely old house at the end of the houses next to the turnpike?

2. What positive qualities do you overlook in yourself?

3.   What personal assets do others notice in you?

Fuel for Thought: You may not know the answer to question #3 until you ask people who know you. Bannink (2017) outlines an exercise where clients identify three strengths that helped them to reach this point in their profession. They then discuss them with a colleague, after which the client asks the colleague which three assets they would name in the client's professional success.

34. Maps and Global Positioning: Where Do I Go?

When I was a child, I loved to look at maps. I could scan them for hours, examining the name of a town, the size of a city, and the distance from one place to another. The roadways and rivers formed a colorful "spider web," adding to my fascination. Even so, when it came to actually getting into a car for trips, we occasionally would get lost. What to do? Where to go? Should we stop and ask for directions?

Many of those questions were answered by the development of the Global Positioning System (GPS). Almost every challenge of navigation is gone. No more difficulty in unfolding (and refolding—ugh) the paper map stored in the glove compartment. Just turn on the GPS, type or speak your destination, and you're off. Miss a turn? No problem. It will recalibrate and give you another route. It takes all the "destination stress" away!

Life doesn't have a GPS, though many wish it did. But let's think again. Perhaps there is a life GPS—call it a daytimer, a scheduling application on your phone or computer, or a home calendar. It tells you your "directions" for the day. But if you use it too frequently, you risk turning into a "human doing" instead of a "human being," because life becomes a matter of doing, doing and doing. Unfortunately, when life's GPS is cranked on high, the challenging, joyful, and educational events can get lost.

The beauty of life can often be found in the serendipity that it offers. Every day, wonderful things large and small happen, things we did not plan nor expect. If we are operating solely on the GPS mode in life, we would miss them entirely.

<u>Final Tune-Up</u>: A GPS is excellent for efficiency, but the joys of life can often be found in inefficiency.

<u>Questions for Driving Your Life</u>:

1. Have you become dependent on your life GPS? How do you think that happened?

2. Are you using your life GPS too much?

3. How difficult would it be to turn down the volume of your life GPS for 6 hours? A whole day?

<u>Fuel for Thought</u>: Your sense of direction might decline with lack of use, with some studies suggesting that the use of a GPS for even a few hours may impair one's skills for navigation in the short term (Ellard, as cited in Ghose, 2013).

35. Construction and Detours: Who Wants Them?

I used to detest construction and detours. I thought they were a pain in the neck. They slowed me down, sometimes a lot, and constantly having to use the brakes was simply aggravating.

Yet I have started to see them differently, and with that, construction and detours are now things of marvel. Yes, *marvel*. First, construction involves the development of something new, and from a road perspective, newer most often means better. How can you argue with that? Second, what construction teams do is incredible to me. I wouldn't have the faintest idea about how to plan—and then actually build—a road. Their expertise and work, particularly in all types of weather conditions, are admirable.

Finally, there's the detour. Life is full of detours. Call them obstacles, problems or challenges. They foil our plans and interfere with our wants. Or do they *really*? When something gets in the way, consider what a gift it is in challenging our resources, fostering our creativity, teaching us patience, and empowering us to change our perspectives. Life detours are going to happen. Could you imagine how uneventful life would be without them?

<u>Final Tune-Up</u>: Embrace life detours for the gifts they offer.

<u>Questions for Driving Your Life</u>:

1. What are your thoughts about life detours?

2. When is the last time that you had to take an unexpected life detour? How did you face it?

3. What did you *gain* from that experience?

<u>Fuel for Thought</u>: Some of the world's most famous inventions can be considered serendipity accidents, including the discovery of penicillin and the creation of the potato chip (Greenwald, 2018).

36. Keep Left: Driving on the Wrong Side of the Road?

While at a dinner party in England, a new acquaintance asked my wife how she was settling into life in England. "Oh, pretty well," she replied. "It takes some time getting used to things, like driving on the wrong side of the road."

The man was somewhat taken back. "*Wrong* side of the road? But it was we British who invented driving!"

About 75 countries travel on the left side of the road (Hewitt, 2018). If you've ever visited one of them, you are well aware of how unusual it seems if your country drives on the right. According to the same website article, the practice of moving along on the left was common until the 1700s, particularly for feudal societies of mostly right-handed people. Since jousting knights—who were mostly right-handed—carried lances with their right arm, it made sense to pass along the left of someone. That way, if you were passing a stranger along the road, you would have your protective weapon between you and the other person.

Yet a part of the reason that the US drives on the right was to remove any remnants of British ways (2pass, n.d.). Rebellious, wouldn't you say?

Doing something differently can be both enjoyable and discombobulating. It upends our daily routines and can make us view and experience the world differently, teaching us many lessons about ourselves and our life. Go ahead. Try something in the "driving on the left" spirit today. Write with your opposite hand. Go a day without screens. Give a stranger a smile. Write a thank-you note to that favorite teacher from grade school. Think left. Go left. Have a left-handed day (even if you already are!).

Final Tune-Up: In the spirit of O'Hanlon's (1999) book entitled *Do One Thing Different*, decide to do exactly that today. Expect mild surprises.

Questions for Driving Your Life:
1. Some chase scenes in movies feature cars driving on the left (instead of the right) at high speeds. What is your reaction when watching this?
2. Now slow down the pace. Imagine driving on a country road in England. What would that be like for you?
3. How is it for you to do something the opposite way?

Fuel for Thought: Habits and routines enable us to use a part of the brain that uses little energy. The basal ganglia act like an internal automatic pilot that, once programmed, requires little to no effort from us to accomplish amazing things. So, if tired and running on empty, defaulting to habits can get us through and support happiness (Carter, 2012).

37. Decisions, Decisions, Decisions: Give Yourself Credit

I was 17 years old and riding home with an older brother who was driving. "This driving thing is so easy," I said. He looked at me quizzically. "But you've only driven in parking lots. How do you know?" I explained, "Oh, I just can tell." He immediately pulled the car over, put it in park, got out of the car, and told me, "OK, smart guy, you drive."

I was flabbergasted, but confident enough to think I could do it. After all, I had my driver's permit, which, in the mind of a teen, gave me the notion that I was a relative expert behind the steering wheel. I made it home, but was petrified. Were there any cars coming at that stop sign? Was I going too fast (or too slow)? When should I use my turn signal?

Think about the complexity of driving for a moment. If you were to describe the act of driving to aliens from another planet, it would sound overwhelming. Drivers are constantly processing information from both inside and outside of the car and making corresponding decisions, often without seemingly giving it a second thought. So many factors go into driving, including weather conditions, the speed of other vehicles, and traffic signs. Determining what to pay attention to can be complicated when there is a crying baby in the backseat, a song you dislike playing on the radio, oncoming traffic, and debris blowing across your lane. What do you do first? These decisions are quite complicated. On top of it all, add cell phones, and it's a wonder that drivers make it to their destinations at all!

Life is packed with the same moments of taking in multiple pieces of information and making decisions. We do it hundreds, if not thousands, of times every day. Take something as simple as the clothes that you decide to wear in the morning. It may depend on a number of different things, such as the weather forecast, your activities that day, what clothes are clean, or your mood. And this is just one decision! Imagine the amount of data your brain processes each minute of each day.

Ever made a bad decision? Sure, everyone looks back and says that about some choice in life. However, look at all of the successful choices you made, particularly when you think of how many decisions you made in total. Instead of dwelling on those not-so-great decisions—and then feeling guilty, depressed, or regretful—focusing on the positive decisions brings a different mindset. Hey, if you made some good decisions in the past, you can surely do the same today, tomorrow and in the future.

Final Tune-Up: Decisions: bad ones are a part of life. Know that many good ones have been made and *will* be made, too.

Questions for Driving Your Life:

1. What bad decision actually ended up being a good one?
2. Name three good decisions that you recently made. How did you make them?
3. How often do you give yourself credit, a pat on the back, for making good decisions?

Fuel for Thought: A writer for *The Boston Globe* saved $12,000 in just three years by making the decision to save every $5 bill she acquired (Franklin, 2008).

38. Car Talk: Laughter

I bet that Tom and Ray (aka "Click and Clack," the Tappet Brothers of the former National Public Radio show, *Car Talk*) never dreamt of how successful their venture would be when they started their program. What a wonderful show it was, too! Between their knowledge, creativity, and self-deprecating humor, they even attracted a listener like me who knows so little about cars.

And which of those qualities is most important? That's easy, at least for me: the humor. They don't take themselves too seriously and often laugh at themselves. What an attribute to have. Being able to laugh at yourself sends at least three key messages: a) you realize that you are not perfect, b) you take the time to laugh and realize how beneficial that is, and c) you are communicating that life is meant to be funny at times. Sure, it has serious times and moments, but I don't think it is designed to be that way all of the time.

By the way, the gift of laughing at oneself doesn't equate to having low self-esteem. In fact, I would contend that getting a chuckle out of one's actions is a mark of solid self-esteem in realizing that we are not robots and that some things we do are simply odd enough to deserve a smile. Ever look for your glasses, only to realize that they are on top of your head? You get the picture.

Final Tune-Up: Go ahead and get a laugh at your own expense.

Questions for Driving Your Life:

1. What things do you do that strike you as funny?
2. Picture someone who takes life too seriously. How would you describe them?
3. How can a self-deprecating, humorous approach work for you?

Fuel for Thought: Who knew that laughter releases nitric oxide in the body? This aids the body in decreasing clotting and blood pressure. According to cardiologist Dr. Michael Miller, a good sense of humor can be a fine way to "relieve stress and anxiety and bring back a sense of normalcy during these turbulent times" (Schiffman, 2020).

39. We're Drivers, not Cars: People Instead of Labels

Picture this scenario: You're driving on a major highway when, unexpectedly, another car suddenly enters your lane, causing you to immediately hit the brakes to avoid an accident. Then you find yourself instantly yelling, "Hey, what's that car doing?"

A similar pattern arises when describing a car race, a soapbox derby, or a tractor trailer event. The focus is on the car—the vehicle—and not the person inside who is driving it. We refer to the "green Mercedes that was going 80 miles per hour" instead of the "driver going 80 miles per hour." We refer to "the crazy van" swerving back and forth along the road instead of the person driving it.

What's the point? Really, it's the driver doing the thing, not the thing itself. It's the person, not the car.

Many of us do the same thing in life. Ever hear someone refer to the "addict" who was violent or the "foreigner" who wasn't fluent in English or the "hippie" or the "Gen Xer." Sometimes we just don't like talking about people as *people*.

Taken one step further, notice the types of labels we use to describe people. They are often derogatory, demeaning and inferior, as if to distance *us* from *them*.

We're all sharing the same "road of life" with everyone going to their respective destination.

Final Tune-Up: Labels are misleading. We're people, not things.

Questions for Driving Your Life:

1. Think about a recent time when you referred to a label instead of a person. When did it occur? What was the meaning of the label?

2. Have you ever been described as a label? What was your reaction?

3. Without any labels, how might you view others differently?

Fuel for Thought: It can be difficult to shake off a label someone else has put on. Primacy effects—the tendency for early impressions of others having excessive weight in our thinking—can be the problem. If you wonder why your parents still treat you as if you were 12 years old, think primacy effect (Halvorson, 2015). As she observed, "In their eyes, you are still the person they first knew you to be—naïve, inexperienced, and more than a little foolish" (p. 25).

40. Double-parking: Life in the City

Double-parking—parking next to a car that is already parked parallel to the curb—is common in some cities because of the shortage of spaces, particularly on side streets. The necessity of it is evident in emergencies, when someone is rushed, or in temporary situations. However, it can incredibly inconvenient when you are the one who's car is blocked in, preventing you from departing.

I remember an episode of *Seinfeld* (David, Seinfeld, & Leifer, 1994), where George and Kramer exit a shop, only to find their car trapped by a double-parked car. George explodes with anger, particularly after finding no note of explanation on his car. In a later scene where they continue to wait in the dark, George's anger and impatience shift into high gear. He goes on another tirade at this point, complaining about the stupidity and total lack of consideration of drivers who double-park in classic (and hilarious) George Costanza fashion. He is adamant that double-parking is how dictators get their start before venting, "If I were running for office, I would ask for the death penalty for double-parkers" in only the way that George's thinking could escalate.

Final Tune-Up: Sometimes life finds us blocked with no *apparent* alternatives. The key word is "apparent."

Questions for Driving Your Life:

1. Place yourself in George's spot. What would you do when faced with a similar situation? What thoughts go through your mind?

2. Now reverse the situation. Have you ever had to double-park, and, in the process, blocked another driver?

3. When blocked in by a driver who has double-parked, do you take the time to consider creative alternatives?

Fuel for Thought: Instead of getting angry, try to smile. A study at the University of Kansas revealed that when people smiled through stress-provoking tasks, they appeared to have less stress. The phrase "grin and bear it" may be a way to experience health-related benefits (U.S. News & World Report, 2012).

Behavior

41. Accelerators: Choose Your Speed

This device is brilliant. Press the accelerator and the car goes faster. Take your foot off of it and the car inevitably slows down. It's that simple, and it works the same on go-carts, bumper cars, and large trucks.

You choose how quickly or slowly you want to proceed. Society even has labels for that. Are you a "lead foot?" Have you been told that you drive like a "little ol' granny?"

It is analogous to reality therapy, which includes the notion of choice theory and the idea that our behavior is driven by five needs (survival; love and belonging; power; freedom; and fun). Adler also had the same concept in believing that behavior is teleological or goal-oriented. Once again, the driver chooses the speed.

I recall a client during my training…for the first few sessions, he entered the room, sat down, and talked for what seemed to be an endless 50 minutes. I found it impossible to get a word into our exchange. At the end of the session, he would often thank me for what he was gaining from counseling. I left the session grateful for the comment, but utterly baffled about what had taken place. I felt like a dog chasing a car, a venture that would inevitably fail. From a process standpoint, I was exhausted.

Finally, in the next session, I broke the pattern. "Hey, I've noticed something," I started and then explained the previous sessions. "It's as if you're going 65 miles per hour, but I'm going 25 miles an hour." The analogy worked. He got it entirely, and the session went much differently, resulting in greater depth and outcome.

Here's a final thought: Anxiety can produce faster speeds. Depression can result in slower speeds.

<u>Final Tune-Up</u>: It's *your* accelerator. You get to select your speed.

<u>Questions for Driving Your Life</u>:

1. What is your life speed right now? What is dictating your choice in speed?

2. What would you like your life speed to be? How would that be different for you?

3. Are there any reasons to slow down or speed up as you see the road ahead?

<u>Fuel for Thought</u>: Some tips for navigating a fast-paced life include 1) taking time for a few deep breaths, giving the brain extra oxygen to not only feel calmer, but to also feel more energized; and 2) focusing your attention to what you feel grateful for to reduce frazzle-fueled thoughts while shifting to happier ones (McLeod, 2011).

42. Speeding Ticket: Trying to Change Behavior

I suspect that a fair number of people reading this sentence have gotten a speeding ticket at some point. Yes, they are not fun. Getting pulled over, the police car siren on, people driving by thinking to themselves, "Gosh, I'm sure glad that's not me." You know the scene and see it nearly every day. Then comes the worst part: having to pay the (often hefty) fine. Ugh.

Speeding tickets are designed to change driving behavior. No one wants to get one; no one wants to pay a fine, regardless of the amount. Yet many people are willing to consistently drive over the speed limit in hopes they will avoid such a ticket.

Life abounds with speeding tickets with varying consequences. Students' bad behavior results in staying after school. Paying a bill after its due date means an extra charge, intended to teach you to pay future expenses on time. Committing a felony may translate into jail time as a way to punish someone who breaks the law.

Part of the question is whether the consequence teaches one a lesson about changing behavior. I have known people who got a speeding ticket, only to get another one the following month. I have known of others who received a ticket, never to get one again in their driving careers.

Final Tune-Up: Life has speeding tickets intended to help people change, but they are not always successful.

Questions for the Client:

1. Have you ever gotten a speeding ticket in life that tells you to slow down? This could be anything from a partner saying you are doing too much to suffering a mild heart attack.

2. If the fine (behavioral consequence) wasn't enough to change your behavior, what would be a suitable fine that would prompt you to look at your behavior?

3. Instead of a penalty such as a ticket, what kind of reward might motivate you to change?

Fuel for Thought: With *limits* in mind, are you trying to find ways to alleviate those temptations for less-than-healthy foods? Consider these ideas: chewing gum, distracting yourself, or storing the food that you crave outside of the house (The Mayo Clinic, 2021).

43. High Beams: Illuminating the Path Ahead

I was about eight years old, and we were driving home late one evening from a nearby town. My 21-year-old brother was driving while I sat in the passenger seat, and I was observing his use of the high beams. They seemed to magically turn themselves off and on as a car approached us and then passed into the distance. My brother wasn't turning any switch, and it happened repeatedly. "How do the headlights do that?" I wondered aloud. "Oh, that," my brother said. "I just do that with my brain. If I want them to turn off, I just think it and it happens." As soon as he said that, a car approached and off went the high beams. "See, just like that," he said.

I was amazed. My mother, sitting in the back seat, laughed and said, "Pat, you can't do that to your little brother." He came clean: There was a switch on the floor, undetectable to me, that he could operate with his foot! If it weren't for my mother, I may have still believed him.

High beams are a wonderful tool for seeing greater distances in dark places. It's the bionic eyes of a car. In other facets of life, we have binoculars and telescopes, but high beams are different because they light our path so that we can navigate our way. Without them, seeing our way would be much harder.

Wouldn't it be great to have high beams in life, too? Something that would let us see further down the road than we normally can? Guess what? You do, at least to a certain extent. Connecting reality therapy to the high beams analogy—you choose your behavior. That means that you choose your direction based on your goals. In other words, if you wanted to drive from Topeka to Kansas City, you can choose the route based on your goal. One way will get you there in the shortest amount of time, while another road might offer nice scenery. Turning on your high beams allows you to look ahead with greater clarity.

Final Tune-Up: The behavior that a person chooses can light their path toward longer-term goals.

Questions for Driving Your Life:

1. Have you used your life high beams in the past with success?

2. Turn on your life high beams and look further down the road. What do you see yourself doing in the coming months?

3. Sometimes high beam bulbs burn out. Do yours need to be replaced?

Fuel for Thought: Self-efficacy, a term describing an individual's belief in his/her ability to accomplish something, affects the level of commitment to goals and not giving up in the face of obstacles (Maddux & Gosselin, 2003).

44. Hot and Cold Air Conditioning: Comfort Controls

Think about the joy of getting into your car first thing on a cold winter morning, turning on the heat, and being able to forget about the freezing temperatures outside your vehicle. Growing up in the frigid winters in Western New York, I developed an appreciation for car heaters. Move that dial to the big red area and, within minutes, it was as comfortable as could be. Not to mention the new feature on some cars which is just heavenly—car seat heaters which warm the cushion and the driver.

Conversely, imagine a car without heating/cooling units and how horrible it would be. Driving a car in Florida *without* air conditioning? I did (what was I thinking?), and it was brutal. Thirty seconds in there any time after April 1 was analogous to sitting for an hour in a sauna.

Because we spend so much time in our cars, comfort—specifically the air temperature—is important. Similarly, in life, we want to avoid constantly living at the boiling point of anger or in the coldness of depression. I think we have all seen a person move from a state of calmness to outrage in just a few moments.

So then, what do you do to regulate your emotions? How do you turn up your emotional energy or cool off your feelings? Some ideas are: music to soothe (or to dance!); talking to friends (to vent or to listen for input); taking a walk (to release stress or increase energy); or simply laughing (to cool off or heat up).

<u>Final Tune-Up</u>: Choosing good ways to self-regulate is a part of emotional health.

<u>Questions for Driving Your Life</u>:

1. What healthy ways do you use to control your life temperature? Any unhealthy ways?

2. Picture someone who is good at self-regulating emotions. How do they do it?

3. Choose one new (and healthy) way to self-regulate and try it for a few days. How did it work?

<u>Fuel for Thought</u>: Smells can have a powerful emotional effect. Olfactory receptors are linked to the limbic system, the most primitive part of the brain and also believed to be the seat of emotion. Just hearing about a pleasant aroma can elicit an emotional response equal to or greater to experiencing it (Fox, 1999).

45. Spinning My Wheels: Frustrating!

What a terrific idiom that comes straight from driving: "spinning my wheels." Whether it is in snow or mud, spinning wheels can be maddening. Your car is stuck, and you certainly don't want it to be where it is. But whether the accelerator is slightly pressed or pushed to the floor, the wheels simply can't gain the traction they need to move the car.

Some people find their lives fitting this phrase. They seem to be "spinning their wheels" whether it be in their love lives, work lives, or family lives Nothing seems to work. If you've experienced this, you can probably relate to the chorus of this song by Dada (1998): "And I'd love to be happy / I forget how it feels / Driving towards somewhere / Instead of spinning my wheels."

When your wheels are spinning, nothing seems to work. You try, you try again, and the same results happen. I often find that, when my wheels spin, there are two things to consider: 1) My wheels work. That is, they are functioning properly. It's just my location that's bad. 2) I am trying the same solutions time after time after time. It's reminiscent of the saying, "Craziness is trying the same thing over and over and expecting different results."

I also recall a piece of life wisdom someone gave me a long time ago: If you lost something, stop looking for it. I don't know about you, but when I lose something (and it happens all too often), I tend to look in the same places repeatedly. Now reread the definition of craziness in the previous paragraph. Trying the same things over and over—spinning one's wheels—is not effective.

Final Tune-Up: Spinning your wheels in life is a sign that your wheels are working and a different approach might be needed.

Questions for Driving Your Life:

1. Think about the last time you were spinning your wheels in life. How did you get out of the rut?

2. Do you think you are currently spinning your wheels in life?

3. Pretend you are your own best friend. What input would you give yourself about your life's spinning wheels?

Fuel for Thought: Breaking out of a rut may involve disrupting cues that trigger habits. For example, to disrupt overeating, you might use smaller plates with small helpings to break the cue to overeat.

Successfully breaking a rut means replacing it with a healthier, more desirable habit (Klemm, 2013).

46. Rental Cars: A Different "You" for a Short Time

Many drivers have at some point used a rental car, perhaps while their car was being repaired or when they were on a trip. It's rather fun, isn't it? Drivers get to choose the make and model of their temporary car. From subcompact to luxury, the selections are fun to consider.

Upon sitting in a rental for the first time, drivers have to get settled, adjust the seats and mirror, and find out how to do things like turn on the radio and open the trunk. With that "new car" smell and streak-free windows, it's a wonderful feeling to drive away in your "new" temporary vehicle.

As I think about rental cars, my mind goes to an intervention from Adlerian counseling. This activity asks people to pretend they possess a certain desirable quality that, at the moment, they may lack. "Acting as if" can be a very good strategy to move toward change. Lack confidence? Take some time each day and act as if you have abundant confidence. Indecisive? Block out a couple of hours and be a decisive person. Unmotivated? Start acting tomorrow as a highly motivated individual.

Rental cars allow us to "act as if." They are temporary ways to move about differently and to have—at least for a while—the quality that you want.

Final Tune-Up: Try a life rental car and experience being different in a way that you desire.

Questions for Driving Your Life:

1. What qualities would you want from a temporary life rental car? (Start small.)

2. How do you think you might be different after using this life rental car for a few minutes? Hours? Days?

3. What would it cost you for this temporary experience?

Fuel for Thought: As kids, we used costumes and dress-up games to try being like someone else. As it turns out, playing dress up may help kids to develop empathy as they walk in others' shoes. Kids who participated in role play were found to have greater ability in judging the feelings of others (Parenting, n.d.).

47. Awareness Courses: Go Learn!

While living in England, I read a newspaper article about drivers caught speeding in Cambridgeshire. They had the option of taking a "speed awareness" course in order to avoid penalty points. The article said the cost of these courses had risen from 60 GBP to 87 GBP (about $140 at that time), and the money raised from these courses was enough to purchase 69 cameras throughout the county to catch drivers who are speeding ("Speeding drivers finance cameras," 2011).

I am certain that many walking into such courses are not happy about the prospect of taking it in the first place. Yet, I wonder how those same drivers feel as they leave. What gems—as small as they might seem—are they taking from the course? And how might these gems change their driving?

I think of such courses as professional development for drivers. Sure, they are somewhat mandatory, but nonetheless, they educate drivers and aim to change their habits behind the wheel.

Professional development is becoming more popular for both occupational and personal reasons, leading to expanding job possibilities and personal growth. A variety of personal development courses are featured by local school districts or community colleges. Ever wanted to speak Thai? Cook Russian food? Improve your public speaking skills? Taking a course along the way, for fun or for professional gains, can be the equivalent of the "awareness courses" that some drivers opt to take.

Final Tune-Up: Education is a lifelong endeavor that can be both enriching and enjoyable.

Questions for Driving Your Life:

1. Write down two things you would like to learn for fun or for your job. Why would you like to pursue them?

2. Find the adult education catalogue for your local school district or community college. In which courses might you be interested?

3. Imagine you have gained the skill from the desired course. How would you/your life be different?

Fuel for Thought: Have you ever met someone who can never quite say, "I don't know"? They probably aren't a lifelong learner, according to Georgianna Sergakis, PhD, an associate professor at The Ohio State University. Dr. Sergakis described lifelong learners as those individuals "who readily admit that they do not know it all," adding that they possess the drive to add to their existing knowledge base (Bunch, 2020).

48. Roundabouts: Is Life One of Them?

My friend turned on his GPS as we prepared to drive to our destination. The voice of the GPS, however, was different than the female voice with the British accent to which I was accustomed while in the US. This voice was a male with a Southern accent. This made me chuckle. We were driving in England and it just seemed odd to hear that voice in this context.

But it didn't stop there. On the way, we encountered about 12 roundabouts, which are fairly common in the UK. As we approached a roundabout, the GPS voice would say, "Stay left, stay left on this do-thingy." Do-thingy? That was the name for the roundabout.

Those "do-thingys," similar to the revolving doors found as you enter some buildings, can be rather confusing. An online search of roundabout videos will uncover the challenge that drivers can have in trying to navigate them successfully. Some drivers are likely perplexed, wondering when or how to enter or exit the traffic circle properly.

Does life ever feel like you're driving around in circles? Doing the same old thing? Routine? Job? Home? What's worse is getting off that roundabout. Which way should you go and is it the right direction? If you're on such a revolving journey in life, you may wonder how in the world you got caught in such a rut. However, look on the bright side: At least you're moving.

Final Tune-Up: Recognizing your repetitive thinking and behavior patterns can be a first step toward changing them.

Questions for Driving Your Life:

1. Describe your roundabout in life. What is it like? How did you get there in the first place?

2. How will you successfully get off of the life roundabout? Do you need to change speeds? Do you need to use your turn signal and communicate with others (see #22)?

3. Imagine you are a driver on the roundabout watching a car go around incessantly. What might you do to help? How would that translate to life?

Fuel for Thought: Looking for rut-breaking ideas? Bridges (2017) offered seven methods, including exercise, avoiding perfectionism, and making lists as a way to break something into steps.

49. Car Radios: Ability to Change Frequencies

As a boy, I was amazed at how quickly one of my older brothers was able to change radio stations while driving. He had the quickest radio fingers in New York State! If he didn't like the song on one station, he would rapidly switch to a different station. An ad playing on that station? Before you could even mutter "ugh," he'd be on a third station in nanoseconds, all while driving. As a 10-year-old, I was in awe of his talent.

Yet what a wonderful metaphor in the making. The first car radio came along in 1930 (Berkowitz, 2010). The choice in stations today is striking. The number and specialty of stations enables a driver to be listening to 1960s rock one moment, then classical music a moment later, and an all-news station after that.

Imagine if we could change our thinking mode in the same way. From a cognitive therapy perspective, people's thinking affects their feelings and behavior. Consider a situation in which you're feeling sad, anxious, confused, or guilty and then take a moment to identify the thoughts that may be swirling around in your mind. Wouldn't it be remarkable if people could alter their thinking in the same way that they can change the car radio, changing the radio frequency in their mind?

After all, listening to the same station—and thinking similar thoughts—each day would be boring, wouldn't it?

Final Tune-Up: You have a choice in your thinking, much like you choose the radio station in your car.

Question for Driving Your Life:

1. Would you buy a car that offered only one radio station? In a similar way, would you care to use only one thinking station day after day?

2. What is a recent situation where you discovered that modifying your thinking helped you?

3. Consider changing thinking stations the next time you're feeling an emotion that you wanted to shift. How might you do this?

Fuel for Thought: The word "broadcasting" originated from the agricultural industry, as in seeds were "broadcasted" on ground that had been plowed (Fun Trivia, 2021.).

50. H. Nelson Jackson: The Epitome of Persistence

I was feeling bored during a trans-Atlantic flight so I scanned the video offerings. I had already watched a few movies and wondered if anything entertaining might be left. I stumbled upon what turned out to be a fascinating documentary: the story of H. Nelson Jackson. (No, I had never heard of him, either.) A physician from the San Francisco Bay Area, Dr. Jackson became the first person to drive across the continental states, a journey that others had previously tried, but failed to complete. With no prior experience in anything related to this venture, he purchased a 1903 Winton touring car, named it "Vermont" (his home state), and along with mechanic Sewall K. Crocker, successfully made the trip eastward in 63 days. His adventure took him through mountain passes, railroad tracks, and rivers, and in the end, cost him $8,000. While in Idaho, the two men acquired "Bud," a bulldog who was featured in many pictures that chronicled the journey (National Museum of American History, n.d.).

It's a grand story that features confidence, dedication, patience (with frequent breakdowns), creativity, and passion. Imagine the fortitude that the two men must have had in planning then implementing the venture. Others had tried it before, but without success. The side story of Bud was a perfect cap to the story, adding a caring, humorous element. Jackson and Crocker had even purchased goggles for Bud to keep the dust out of his eyes. Could you picture that bulldog with flight goggles cruising across America? How hilarious that must have been!

I end this book with the story of Jackson and Crocker because of its inspirational ingredients for life: taking risks, interpersonal (and interspecies!) connections, teamwork, love (apparently Jackson sent many such letters to his wife along the way), goal-setting and overcoming numerous challenges. So much of what they did can be applied to life!

Final Tune-Up: If your car breaks down in life, think of Jackson and Crocker and keep on keeping on.

Questions for Driving Your Life:

1. How does the story of Jackson and Crocker inspire you?

2. What do you think was the hardest part of their journey and how does that relate to your life?

3. What life venture would you like to set for yourself?

Fuel for Thought: Adopting an adventurous outlook can enhance everyday experiences in life, such as cooking a new recipe you never tried before, taking a different path to work, or approaching someone at work you might have been afraid to talk to before. Confidence can develop by going beyond your normal boundaries in life every day (Delaney, 2008).

Acknowledgments

ENGINES THAT DROVE THIS BOOK

I started to write the first edition of this book while on sabbatical at the University of Cambridge, and I thank my wife, Susanna, for her patience and support then and now. Melissa Lake, a Licensed Professional Counselor in Indiana, Pennsylvania, and a graduate of the Department of Counseling at Indiana University of Pennsylvania, has been a tremendous collaborator with her research and writing skills in formulating segments that accompany the metaphors.

The organizational and conceptual skills of my former graduate assistants at Indiana University of Pennsylvania were extremely beneficial for this book. I thank all of the students with whom I have had the pleasure of learning over the course of my career. They have been exceptionally inspiring to me.

Finally, I offer my appreciation to Barbara Dee with Suncoast Digital Press, Inc. Her guidance has been exceptional, both in this project and with my other book, *The Innovator Next Door: 50 Stories of Creative Inspiration to Spark New In-the-Box Thinking* (2020).

About the Authors

John McCarthy has been fascinated with creative thinking and problem-solving since childhood. Inspired by seven older siblings, he learned the art and science of practical jokes early in life. His interest in the "outside the ordinary" extended to the playground where friends quickly improvised plays in football huddles, devised trick shots on the basketball court, and found unusual ways to throw a whiffle ball from a pitcher's mound.

He abandoned his dream of playing second base for the Boston Red Sox after high school and instead pursued a degree in mass communication from St. Bonaventure University. He subsequently earned his doctoral degree in Counseling Psychology from the University of Missouri, Kansas City.

He has had the pleasure of being in the university classroom for over 25 years, starting with a two-year stint at National Chengchi University in Taiwan. John served as an academic visitor at the University of Cambridge in Spring 2011 and has offered professional presentations on creativity thinking and other mental health-related topics in Turkey, Singapore, Ukraine, Kyrgyzstan, Malaysia, China, Hong Kong, England, Canada, and Taiwan.

John has over 30 journal publications and over 60 professional presentations. His professional writings have been featured in the *Huffpost.com*, *Pittsburgh Post-Gazette*, the *Buffalo News, Cleveland. com, Counseling Today*, and the *Psychotherapy Networker*. He wrote *The Innovator Next Door: 50 Stories of Creative Inspiration to Spark New In-the-Box Thinking* (2020, Suncoast Digital Press).

In his sixth decade, he hopes to hike in Indonesia and Uganda, host a show on PBS, study improv and Mandarin, and continue to marvel at others' creative stories. His blogs can be found at creativestrengths.com.

Other books by John McCarthy

The Innovator Next Door:
50 Stories of Creative Inspiration to Spark New In-the-Box Thinking
(2020)

Melissa Lake, M.A., a Licensed Professional Counselor, specializes in general mental health counseling for individuals recovering from anxiety, depression, and grief. She offers a client-centered approach emphasizing compassion, self-discovery, growth and potential at her private practice in Indiana, PA.

References

2pass. (n.d.). Why we drive on the left in the UK. http://www.2pass.co.uk/goodluck.htm

Dosomething.org. (n.d.) 11 facts about healthy living. (n.d.). https://www.dosomething.org/facts/11-facts-about-healthy-living

Adams, J. (2007, December 19). The unrecognized (and much used) glovebox. NBC News.com. http://www.nbcnews.com/id/22313202/ns/business-autos/t/unrecognized-much-used-glovebox/#.U9z-gLHCe9U

Albright, M. B. (2014, November 5). History of tailgating. *National Geographic*. https://www.nationalgeographic.com/culture/food/the-plate/2014/11/05/history-of-tailgating/

American Psychological Association. (2008). Listening to the warning signs of stress. www.apa.org/news/press/releases/warning-signs.pdf

Ascher, K. & Williams, P. (1979). Movin' right along [Recorded by Jim Henson & Frank Oz]. On *The Muppet Movie, Original Soundtrack Recording*[LP]. Walt Disney Records.

Ariga, A., & Lleras, A. (2011). Brief and rare mental "breaks" keep you focused: Deactivation and reactivation of task goals preempt vigilance decrements. *Cognition, 118*(3), 439-443.

Autoeurope. (n.d.). Speed limits around the world. https://www.autoeurope.com/travel-blog/speed-limits-around-the-world/

Bannink, F. (2017). *201 positive psychology applications*. W.W. Norton & Company.

Berkowitz, J. (2010, October 25). The history of car radios. *Car & Driver*. http://www.caranddriver.com/features/the-history-of-car-radios

Bernhard, T. (2011, June 16). How to ask for help: learn to communicate skillfully with others so you can get the help you need. *Psychology Today*. http://www.psychologytoday.com/blog/turning-straw-gold/201106/how-ask-help

Biography.com. (2021, June 3). Garrett Augustus Morgan, Sr. http://www.biography.com/people/garrett-morgan-9414691

Bridges, F. 2017, October 31). 6 ways to get out of a rut. *Forbes*. https://www.forbes.com/sites/francesbridges/2017/10/31/6-ways-to-get-out-of-a-rut/?sh=2330f73b77c7

Bunch, D. (2020). AARC members share their take on lifelong learning and why it matters in their careers. *AARC Times, 44*(6), 21–25.

Burns, S. T., Sholtis, H., Lemmer, S., Rauk, I., & Mohamed, Z. (2020). Independently licensed counselors' work values. *Counseling & Values*, *65*(2), 235–252. https://doi-org.proxy-iup.klnpa.org/10.1002/cvj.12140

Carter, B. (2012, September 21). Tailgate parties are a "powerful impulse'" and a microcosm of society. *Wired.* https://www.wired.com/2012/09/anthropology-of-tailgating/

Carter, C. L. (2012). Habits are everything.. *Psychology Today* http://www.psychologytoday.com/blog/raising-happiness/201204/habits-are-everything

Centers for Disease Control and Prevention. (2020b). *Drowsy driving: Asleep at the wheel.*https://www.cdc.gov/sleep/features/drowsy-driving.html

Centers for Disease Control and Prevention (2020a). *Sleep and sleep disorders.* https://www.cdc.gov/sleep/index.html

Chapla, S. (2012, September 6). Not simply a party: Tailgaters contribute to team victory and even university brand, new study shows. *Notre Dame News.* https://news.nd.edu/news/not-simply-a-party-tailgaters-contribute-to-team-victory-and-even-university-brand-new-study-shows/

Chesley, G. L., Gillett, D. A., & Wagner, W. G. (2008). Verbal and nonverbal metaphor with children in counseling. *Journal of Counseling & Development*, *86*(4), 399-411.

Corey, G. (2005). *Theory and practice of counseling and psychotherapy* (7th ed.). Belmont, CA: Brooks/Cole.

Corey, G. (2013). *Theory and practice of counseling and psychotherapy* (9th ed.). Belmont, CA: Brooks/Cole.

Corey, G. (2017). *Theory and practice of counseling and psychotherapy* (10th ed.). Brooks/Cole.

Dada (1998). Spinning my wheels. On *Dada* [Audio CD]. Olympic & Morgan Studios.

David, L., Seinfeld, J., Leifer, C. (Writers), & Cherones, T. (Director). (1994, February 3). The dinner party. *Seinfeld.* Shapiro/West Productions; Castle Rock Entertainment.

Dayton, L. (2010, September 13). Social support network may add to longevity. *Los Angeles Times.* http://articles.latimes.com/2010/sep/13/health/la-he-friends-health-20100913

Delaney, B. (2008, December 19). The spirit of adventure. *CNN.* http://edition.cnn.com/2008/WORLD/europe/03/07/spiritof.adventure/

Drum, K. (2020, April 26). Who invented the phrase "social distancing"? *Mother Jones.* https://www.motherjones.com/kevin-drum/2020/04/who-invented-the-phrase-social-distancing/

Fox, K. (1999). The smell report: An overview of facts and findings. *Social Issues Research Centre.* www.sirc.org/publik/smell.pdf

Franklin, M. (2008, July 20). With a bit of creative saving, $5 can get you at least $12,000. *The Boston Globe*. http://archive.boston.com/business/personalfinance/articles/2008/07/20/with_a_bit_of_creative_savings_5_can_get_you_at_least_12000/

Fun Trivia. (2021, August 13). *Radio history trivia questions*. https://www.funtrivia.com/en/Entertainment/Radio-History-14818_2.html

Futrelle, D. (2020). Can money buy happiness? *Time (The science of happiness)*, pp. 50-57.

Genuchi, M. C., Hopper, B., & Morrison, C. R. (2017). Using metaphors to facilitate exploration of emotional content in counseling with college men. *The Journal of Men's Studies*, *25*(2), 133–149. https://doi-org.proxy-iup.klnpa.org/10.1177/1060826516661187

Ghose, T. (2013, March 11). Why humans get lost. *Livescience*. https://www.livescience.com/27787-why-humans-get-lost.html

Gray, C. (2014, May 16). A history of New York traffic lights. *The New York Times*. https://www.nytimes.com/2014/05/18/realestate/a-history-of-new-york-traffic-lights.html

Greenwald, M. (2018, September 25). 30 life-changing inventions that were totally accidental. *Best Life*. https://bestlifeonline.com/accidental-inventions/

Halvorson, H. G. (2015). *No one understands you and what to do about it*. Harvard Business Review Press.

Headlights.com. (2020, March 10). *What states still require car inspection*.

https://headlights.com/what-states-still-require-car-inspection/

Heckerling, A. (Director). (1985). *National Lampoon's European Vacation* [Film]. National Lampoon; Warner Bros.

Henkel L. A. (2014). Point-and-shoot memories: the influence of taking photos on memory for a museum tour. *Psychological Science*, *25*(2), 396–402. https://doi-org.proxy-iup.klnpa.org/10.1177/0956797613504438

Hewitt, E. (2018, September 6). 15 tips for driving on the left side of the road. *USA Today*. https://www.usatoday.com/story/travel/advice/2018/09/06/driving-left-side-road/1207633002/?utm_source=feedblitz&utm_medium=FeedBlitzRss&utm_campaign=usatodaycomtravel-topstories

Huffman, J. P. (2013, July 29). The 100 greatest movie and TV cars of all time. *Edmunds*. https://www.edmunds.com/car-reviews/features/the-100-greatest-movie-and-tv-cars-of-all-time.html

Inoue, K., Hashioka, S., & Takeshita, H. (2020). Tailgating (aori-unten): A recent major social issue in Japan. *Medicine, Science, and the Law*, *60*(3), 234. https://doi-org.proxy-iup.klnpa.org/10.1177/0025802420917063

Jabr, F. (2013, October 15). Why your brain needs more downtime. *Scientific American.* http://www.scientificamerican.com/article/mental-downtime/

Kita, J. and the staff of Reader's Digest Magazine (2012). *Health...The Reader's Digest Version.* The Reader's Digest Association, Inc.

Klemm, W. R. (2013, April 19). Getting out of a rut: Break bad habits. *Psychology Today website.* http://www.psychologytoday.com/blog/memory-medic/201304/getting-out-rut-break-bad-habits

Kopp, R. R. (1995). *Metaphor therapy: Using client-generated metaphors for psychotherapy.* Brunner/Mazel.

Kulik, B. (Director). (1971). *Brian's song* [Film]. Screen Gems Television.

Lloyd, D. (2010, August 23). 5 ways talk therapy can help you. *Huffington Post Healthy Living.* http://www.huffingtonpost.com/delia-lloyd/5-ways-talk-therapy-can-h_b_686825.html

Maddux, J.E., & Gosselin, J. T. (2003). Self-efficacy. In M.R. Leary & J.P. Tangney (Eds.), *Handbook of self and identity.* Guilford.

Maltarich, S. (2021, February 20). Colorado town's outreach aims to save skiers' lives. NPR.org. https://www.npr.org/2021/02/20/969703418/colorado-towns-outreach-aims-to-save-skiers-lives

Mangold, S., & Zschau, T. (2019). In search of the "Good Life": The appeal of the tiny house lifestyle in the USA. *Social Sciences, 8*(1), 26. http://dx.doi.org.proxy-iup.klnpa.org/10.3390/socsci8010026

Marino, G. (2019, December 17). Are you listening? *The New York Times.* https://www.nytimes.com/2019/12/17/opinion/art-of-listening.html?searchResultPosition=3

Marshall, S. (2012, April 5). You are what you wear. *ABC News.* https://abcnews.go.com/blogs/health/2012/04/05/you-are-what-you-wear

The Mayo Clinic. (2021). *Beat your cravings: 8 effective techniques.* https://diet.mayoclinic.org/diet/eat/beat-your-cravings?xid=nl_MayoClinicDiet_20171109

McCarthy, J. (2000, October). Driver's education=Counseling techniques? *Counseling Today*, pp. 7, 29.

McLeod, L. E. (2011, Nov 19). How to enjoy your life even when you can't slow down. *Huffington Post.* https://www.huffpost.com/entry/enjoy-fast-paced-life_b_1116910

Merriam-Webster. (n.d.). *Tailgate noun.* https://www.merriam-webster.com/dictionary/tailgate

Meyers, T. R. (2018, May 10). Why our facial expressions don't reflect our feelings. *BBC Future.* https://www.bbc.com/future/article/20180510-why-our-facial-expressions-dont-reflect-our-feelings

Minnesota Department of Transportation. (n.d.). *Tailgating frequently asked questions.*

Morin, A. (2018, May 28). *3 ways to declutter your mind.* https://www.psychologytoday.com/us/blog/what-mentally-strong-people-dont-do/201805/3-ways-declutter-your-mind

Motavalli, J. (2020, December 31). Look but don't touch: Supercars that have barely been driven. *The New York Times.* https://www.nytimes.com/2020/12/31/business/low-mileage-supercars-lamborghini.html

National Museum of American History (n.d.). *Crossing the country: Somewhere in Wyoming 1903.* Retrieved from http://amhistory.si.edu/onthemove/exhibition/exhibition_7_2.html.

Neugarten, B. L. (1979). Time, age, and the life cycle. *The American Journal of Psychiatry, 136*(7), 887-894.

O'Hanlon, B. (1999). *Do one thing different: Ten simple ways to change your life.* Harper-Collins.

Parenting. (n.d.). Why kids love to play dress-up. http://www.parenting.com/article/why-kids-love-to-play-dress-up.

Parker-Pope, T. (2021, May 27). Day 9: Hug (just a little) longer! *The New York Times.* https://www.nytimes.com/2021/05/27/well/pandemic-wellness-hugging.html

Perlberg, S. (2020, March 7). Germany's freedom from speed limits may be running out of road. *Fortune.* https://fortune.com/2020/03/07/germany-autobahn-speed-limits-green-party/

Project for Public Spaces. (2008, December 31.). Traffic calming techniquespu. http://www.pps.org/reference/livememtraffic/

Ransom, K. (2009, July 22). The 10 best songs about cars. *CNN.* http://www.cnn.com/2009/LIVING/wayoflife/07/22/aa.top.10.car.songs/index.html

Rath, T. (2013). *Eat move sleep: How small changes lead to big changes.* Missionday.

Robert, T., & Kelly, V. A. (2010). Metaphor as an instrument for orchestrating change in counselor training and the counseling process. *Journal of Counseling & Development, 88*(2), 182-188.

Rust, D., & Strauss, M. (n.d.). *What is a milestone?* http://www.ars.usda.gov/SP2UserFiles/Subsite/sciQualRev/Milestones.pdf

Savage, M. (2020, February 14). The housing project where young and old must mingle. BBC.com. https://www.bbc.com/worklife/article/20200212-the-housing-project-where-young-and-old-must-mingle

Schiffman, R. (2020, October 2). Laughter may be effective medicine for these trying times. *The New York Times.* https://www.nytimes.com/2020/10/01/well/mind/laughter-may-be-effective-medicine-for-these-trying-times.html

Seppala, E.M. (2012, October 1). Reading bodies, touching minds—How eye contact, facial expressions, and body language are the key to connection. http://ccare.stanford.edu/psychology-today/reading-bodies-touching-minds-how-eye-contact-facial-expressions-and-body-language-are-the-key-to-connection/

Snyder, C.R., Rand, K.L., & Sigmon, D.R. (2002). Hope theory: A member of the positive psychology family. In C.R. Snyder & S.J. Lopez (Eds.), *Handbook of positive psychology* (pp.257-276). Oxford.

"Speeding drivers finance cameras." (2011, January 27). *Cambridge News*, p. 5

Storlie, C. A., Giegerich, V., Stoner-Harris, T., & Byrd, J. (2018). Conceptual metaphors in internship: Creative journeys in counselor development. *Journal of Creativity in Mental Health*, *13*(3), 331–343. https://doi-org.proxy-iup.klnpa.org/10.1080/15401383.2018.1439790

Tay, D. (2012). Applying the notion of metaphor types to enhance counseling protocols. *Journal of Counseling & Development*, *90*(2), 142-149. doi:10.1111/j.1556-6676.2012.00019.x

Tchassa, K. (2019, September 13). *How do you know it's time to let go?* Medium.com. https://medium.com/swlh/how-do-you-know-its-time-to-let-go-aa7a9a5faec8

Thompson, C. (2019, April). The myth of fingerprints. *Smithsonian Magazine*. https://www.smithsonianmag.com/science-nature/myth-fingerprints-180971640/

Treweek, L. (2020). Treasure boxes: A strategy for encouraging belonging. *Early Childhood Folio*, *24*(1), 26–30.

U.S. Department of Transportation (Bureau of Transportation Statistics). (2018) *Transportation Statistics Annual Report 2018.* Washington, DC.

U.S. News and World Report. (2012). Smile! It might lower your stress level, study shows. http://health.usnews.com/health-news/news/articles/2012/07/31/smile33-it-might-lower-your-stress-level-study-shows

Van Luling, T. (2017, December 6). This is why you get to celebrate your birthday every year. *Huffpost.com*. https://www.huffpost.com/entry/history-of-birthdays_n_4227366?guccounter=1&guce_referrer=aHR0cHM6Ly9kdWNrZHVja2dvLmNvbS8&guce_referrer_sig=AQAAAELZUPIXwJcA_VL-LtaHZH74VZx19EppGoczFx-1VpfM9CAG6XWNJGVKM-38v8RAuK2agttnmRYrW5m7A-r5BwKza66a1tcLHYP6UQ0AKAIz41Jw0GjP-mNESAkqy7KbQ-ZpDvxaRkEGfKQgEhKKJ804wdOf_PcJcmrxsHn-qH4t

Vinney, C. (2019, September 30). *What is the Zeigarnik effect? Definitions and examples.* https://www.thoughtco.com/zeigarnik-effect-4771725

Waldman, M., & Newberg, A. (2012, July 31). The most dangerous word in the world: This word can damage both the speaker's and listener's brain! *Psychology Today.* http://www.psychologytoday.com/blog/words-can-change-your-brain/201207/the-most-dangerous-word-in-the-world

Wansink, B. (2007). *Mindless eating: Why we eat more than we think*. Bantam Books.

Waugaman, E. P. (2011, July 8). Names and identity: The Native American naming tradition. *Psychology Today.* http://www.psychologytoday.com/blog/whats-in-name/201107/names-and-identity-the-native-american-naming-tradition